THE DRAGON'S TRAIL
Wales on Horseback

Paula Brackston

SIGMA
Leisure

Published by Sigma Leisure – an imprint of
Sigma Press, 1 South Oak Lane, Wilmslow, Cheshire SK9 6AR, England.

British Library Cataloguing in Publication Data
A CIP record for this book is available from the British Library.

ISBN: 1-85058-692-6

Typesetting and Design by: Sigma Press, Wilmslow, Cheshire.

Cover Design: The Agency; *cover photograph: Nan Graham*

Printed by: MFP Design & Print

Acknowledgements

My thanks to Bloodaxe Books for permission to reproduce some of R.S. Thomas's work (from "Selected Poems – 1946-1968"), to Peter Lord for kindly allowing me to use a print of one of his beautiful engravings, and to Trek King for their contribution towards our vital equipment.

My gratitude to the following: Jane Morgan, Nikki and Raymond, Major and Mrs Balance, all at the Lluest Trust, Ivor and Jane, Alison Mostyn, Gareth Davies, Anne Ryder-Owen, Mary Baker, Carolyn Morgan, Janet at Foel Farm, Marc Evans, Lizzie and family, Ron at the Black Lion, and all at Fronoleu Farm Hotel. Thank you, also, everyone who assisted us along the way, and family and friends who helped make the trip possible.

I am indebted to Jennie Tierney for her hard work and patience in deciphering and typing my manuscript, and thanks, too, to Cathy Graham for her help with the photographs. A big thank you to Angela for trusting us with Sooty and Holly, without whom this would have been a very long walk!

And a special thank you to Nan Graham, a real friend, who had enough courage and faith to accompany me on the trek – I couldn't have wished for a better ally.

For my mum, Averil Lewis.

Contents

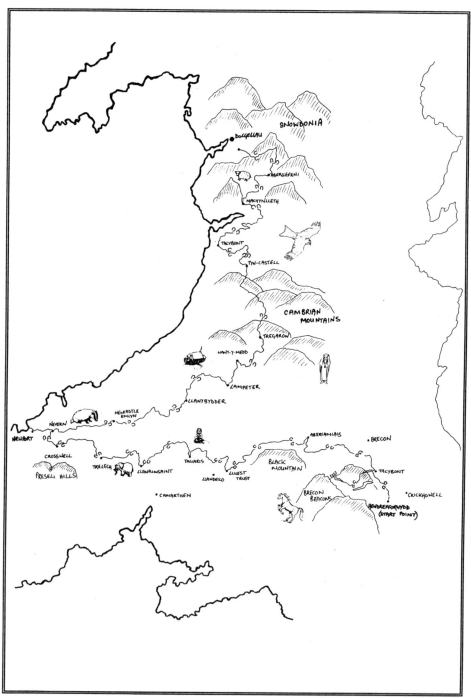

Route of The Dragon's Trail

Day One – How not to do it

'What we need is more baler-twine,' Nan observed as she struggled with Sooty's packs and saddlebags for the first time. This was to be a constant cry from both of us over the next few weeks, along with, 'We should see the village just round the next corner.' Other overused mutterings included, 'There must be a pub around here somewhere,' and 'Bugger!' (The latter being particularly popular when we dropped something.) Certainly, it seems you can never have too much baler-twine. We used it to tie the horses to gates and to secure over-stuffed saddlebags. We wrapped it round parcels of jettisoned items to send home; and we employed works of macramé-like intricacy to anchor vital items of clothing to our packs. It was free yet priceless.

Choosing what to take on a two hundred and fifty-mile trek through Wales when you have to carry everything on the horse you are riding is not easy. Naturally, it being August, one had to be prepared for all weathers, which meant Barbours, waterproof trousers, a warm jumper, tee-shirts, jodhpurs, adequate socks and underwear, riding hat, boots and sandals. A skirt for hot rest days and a scarf and riding gloves were other essentials. Then there were toiletries, a first aid kit, 12 maps, compass, pen knife, pliers/wire cutters, torch, small radio, mobile phone, camera equipment, horses' grooming kit, note pads and pen, money, reflective strips, indispensable parcel tape and so on... Our first attempt at the 'bare minimum' would have required an extra horse. We weeded. Still the saddlebags wouldn't shut. We pruned. At least now we could lift the packs high enough to get them on the horses. Finally we closed our eyes and cast out items purely on the basis of weight. I'm sure serious adventurers would wince at such a system, but I have to say it worked for us. Even if we did end up with three compasses (none of which we ever used) and no Kendal Mint Cakes or guidebook.

Day one was grey and drizzly, which meant we wore more clothes, giving us a false sense of the success of our packing. We tied the horses up in Nan's yard and they stood patiently whilst we fiddled with their tack and loads. After a frantic search for suitable mounts we had struck gold at Llangenny Riding Centre, near Crickhowell. The proprietor, Angela Ralph, envied us our expedition and was happy to find us two stalwart creatures she believed would enjoy the adventure. Holly was clearly designed for the job – a sturdy, 15 hands, chestnut cob cross. Cross what exactly history does not relate, but something had blended with the hardiness of the Welsh cob to refine it a little and add a smidgen of acceleration and enthusiasm. Sooty, a black, 15.2 hands, 90 per cent Dale had all the strength and stamina one could wish for, coupled with a willingness and cheerful disposition that endeared him to us at once.

When it comes to performance, horses can be likened to different makes of car. A Welsh cob is either an old Land Rover or a new Range Rover, depending on which one you get and how many miles there are on the clock. The Thoroughbred is a Porsche among horses – fast, flashy, expensive to keep and justifiably pricey on insurance. An Arab could be seen as a sports car and a Welsh Section A pony as a souped-up Mini.

Nan and I have been friends for twenty years and have spent as much time as opportunity allowed enjoying the challenge of Arab and Thoroughbred types. We both knew, however, that we needed safe, reliable conveyances for this trip and in Holly and Sooty that is what we found.

Nan's home, Hendreforwydd, looks down from its hillside perch on to the attractive little town of Crickhowell. It barely qualifies as a town, having maybe a dozen shops, two schools, and a fire station. In Celtic mythology the Otherworld is the spirit land and home of the gods where time passes to the ticking of a much slower clock than that of the material world. A day in the land of the immortals can signify an entire lifetime for the earthbound. At times I think we can find examples of this surreal timescale in Wales itself. Whereas the people adapt to survive and keep pace with the modern world, the country moves to the heartbeat of a giant, rather than a field mouse. This is obvious in the wild, untouched places, but there is also a sense of it in some of the towns. Crickhowell has changed little in the thirty years I've known it. The butcher will still race from the shop, mid-chop, tearing off his apron, to answer the call of the fire bell. The thirteen pubs still find sufficient custom to keep them going. Was it not on the A40 it would no doubt be even less well known than it is. The A40 is one of my favourite roads, running as it does from London to Ireland, as long as you remember to get on a boat at Fishguard. However, it is a nightmare to ride on, and I had already vowed to avoid doing so at all costs. Holly and Sooty had both come described as 'good in traffic'. Some horses, however, can be better described as good under traffic. I

Setting off

used to ride a Thoroughbred mare who was unfazed by the most monstrous juggernaut, but if she spotted a plastic bag in the hedge she would leap sideways in a heartbeat, under the wheels of the former to avoid the unknown terrors of the latter. There is a certain logic attached to this. Most horses get used to lorries pretty quickly, and come to realise they do not present a threat. As far as the horse is concerned lorries drive round them, not into them. The plastic bag in the hedge, however, is unpredictable. It is a UFO (Unknown Frightening Object). Horses have wide-ranging vision but are not good on detail. The bag could be, and therefore do, anything. It makes sense, then, to put as much distance between you and it as possible. If more drivers understood this they might not tear past clipping stirrup with wing mirror. Unfortunately for all concerned, they are not much interested in the workings of the equine mind and assume that if the animal is safe enough to be ridden on the road it must have the sensibilities of a tractor.

At last we were aboard, packs secured, farewells said to assembled family and friends, including Nan's children, Perdie and Kit, and with hundreds of miles of the unknown ahead of us. I felt a mixture of excitement, anticipation and nervousness. I had planned the trip in a few short weeks and decided not to book accommodation for us for more than a couple of nights ahead at a time, so that we were to trust a great deal to luck and the kindness of strangers.

Our starting point took us along the back road from Llangattock, following the canal to Talybont. Sooty and Holly trotted along happily enough for the first few miles but then spotted a fisherman loading rods and equipment into the back of his car. At this point Sooty decided we had gone far enough and it was best to turn for home. He lurched sideways before running backwards into Holly then refused to move another inch. I urged Holly forward with my heels. Nothing happened. I gave her a smart smack with my whip. No response (probably because I had actually hit the saddlebags). As a last resort I bellowed at her in my best no-nonsense, get-on-with-it-you--silly-mare voice. Reluctantly she edged forward, snorting at the offending fishing rods. The man looked up at us. He was mildly surprised, but continued to rattle and rustle.

'She finds your equipment a bit alarming,' I explained. 'Have you ever had that problem before?'

'No,' he replied, without a smile.

'Miserable bugger,' muttered Nan as we scooted past and continued on our way. Worse terrors lay in wait for the horses. I should point out that Sooty, now thirteen, had arrived at the trekking centre at the age of three and had not left it since. Anything further than five miles from home and not involving carrying total novices on one of the three short routes from his stable was a new experience for him. He was about to be shown a whole new world.

Sadly, riding along the canal path is no longer permitted. It seems slightly ridiculous, given that it was a towpath designed for horses to walk along as they pulled barges. Now, however, tourism has won. Narrow boats are piloted by holidaymakers and the towpath is for walkers. Strategically placed stiles put paid to any plans of a gentle, turfy hack. Still, Sooty would have preferred no contact with the canal at all. At Talybont there is a charming bridge which lifts up to allow boats to pass underneath. Fortunately, it was firmly flat and stationary when we reached it, but it is made of an interesting, rattly surface, which both horses disliked. Just as we thought we were succeeding in persuading them to trust us and cross it, a man appeared carrying a canoe. Holly gave it a long hard stare. Sooty went into reverse gear at high speed. After all, he'd never had a pea green boat waved at him before.

'He seems a bit nervous,' said the boat-wielding man.

'Can't think why,' replied Nan through gritted teeth as she struggled to stop Sooty sitting on a harmlessly parked Renault. Fortunately Holly decided the best escape was in a forwards direction and dashed across the bridge. Sooty followed in a newly invented gait that involved putting his hooves on the terrifying surface as little as possible.

The valley in which the Talybont reservoir lies is wide and peaceful. On one side is a disused railway, which serves as an excellent walking or cycle route, but, again, is impassable on a horse. We found a campsite that provided a good spot to tie up and eat our packed lunch. Nobody took much notice of us. The steady drizzle persisted, making the smell of damp pines so strong I kept thinking of loo cleaner. We studied the map. It was disconcerting to find that by 3pm we had barely covered half of the day's planned route. Steep climbs, a rugged pass through the Brecon Beacons then more roadwork lay between us and Cantref Riding Centre, where we were booked in for the night. Three things were rapidly becoming apparent. First, it's always further than you think, especially if you are measuring the map with a piece of knotted string. Second, it takes longer than you expect to get anywhere, due mainly to time spent tackling hazards, checking the map and readjusting packs. And third, we were already tired and stiff so getting on and off was becoming a major effort. This last point was exacerbated by our packs. Springing into the saddle at the start of a ride is one thing. Heaving yourself aboard a fidgeting horse whilst having to raise your right leg à la Margot Fonteyn to clear the mountain of packs and bundles was quite another. Every gate was greeted with a groan. Incidentally, even on the handiest of all handy pony-class winners only one gate in ten could possibly be opened and closed without getting off.

Riding alongside the reservoir we were treated to some easy bird spotting.

'Coot!' I'd declare.

'Moorhen,' Nan would counter.

'Heron,' I'd announce.

'Buzzard.'

And so on. Buzzards always make me feel at home. I grew up listening to their mewing and watching them soar in circles higher and higher until they disappeared, Icarus-like, into the sun. As for the water itself, it left me strangely untouched. True, the surface shimmered prettily enough under the weak sun which fell between the Paines grey rain clouds, and its silver smoothness worked as an effective foil for the dark, spiky pines and rough green pastures which surrounded it. But I'm with R.S. Thomas on reservoirs – there's something sad and dead about them.

'There are places in Wales I don't go:
Reservoirs that are the subconscious
Of a people, troubled far down
With gravestones, chapels, villages even;
The serenity of their expression
Revolts me, it is a pose
For strangers, a water-colour's appeal
To the mass, instead of the poem's
Harsher conditions.'

Eventually we left the reservoir behind and climbed up the lane which twisted into the Beacons. We were on open mountain now, which meant cattle grids, which meant gates. One attempt to remount Holly brought on a fit of hysterical giggling, weakening me further still. Holly had already assumed the long-suffering expression of someone delivered into the hands of idiots. Nan grabbed me, taking advantage of Sooty's height, and hauled me into the saddle. Our spirits were quickly flattened, however, when we rounded a bend to find yet another cattle grid, and no gate. We stood and stared at it. The fence either side was solid post-and-rail with added wire. My wire cutters were of no use and Red Rum in his prime would have had trouble getting over it. We studied the map again. After curses and oaths we decided this simply could not be the track we were looking for and so trotted on up the road in search of the right one. By now we were all feeling weary. The horses were fitter than we were, but it had already been a long day. The sky had become threateningly grey and the cloud was descending to cloak the very part of the mountain we were riding into. We were well behind schedule too. Nan had been periodically checking her mobile phone and let out a whoop as she finally got a signal on it. The area in which it could send or receive calls was precisely two Sooty lengths. We made a note of the 'phone box' and pressed on. At last we found the right track, or at least the beginning of it. A yellow-cagouled figure, hood up, head down, came towards us. We questioned him about the mountain pass. What it amounted to was that we had about an hour's daylight left to negotiate a steep, stony, narrow track (on one side of which was a terrifying drop) through the Beacons, with visibility down to a few yards because of the cloud. The ride would take a minimum of ninety minutes, assuming we didn't get lost or slip or lame one of the horses. I began to feel the heavy weight of responsibility – Nan and Sooty and Holly were all in this situation because of me. The horses weren't mine, and I had a duty to put their welfare first. Given the conditions, there was a serious risk of injury. I had lived in the mountains long enough to know that the most straightforward of trails can elude one in fog, and in darkness the risk was doubled. I knew if I said we should go on Nan would trust my judgement. She is not reckless, but she's much braver than I am. But I had a responsibility to look after her too, not to mention the fact that she had two young children waiting at home for her, one of them my godson. I made the decision. We would turn back, ride to the 'phone box' and inform those who needed to know of our change of plans. We would have to ride back to the village of Aber and try to find somewhere to spend the night.

To say morale was low would not quite express the weariness with which we turned the horses around and began to retrace our steps. Sooty and Holly, of course, thought it was the most sensible thing we'd done since they met us and strode out keenly towards what they assumed must be home.

After a silent ten minutes I declared I had to have a cigarette. Simple enough, if I wasn't in the habit of smoking roll-ups. I dismounted, looped my arm through the reins and opened my tin. Holly, for reasons we will never know, chose that moment to shake her head violently. The effect was to send tobacco, filters and papers flying in all directions before landing in the mud. Contrary to any precedent, nothing fell on stony ground. Nan and I both let out shrieks that developed into uncontrollable, hysterical laughter. I am still convinced Holly was in league with my mother in an effort to make me give up smoking.

Four gates later we were able to use the phone. The lady who had been expecting us for B&B hours ago was concerned and then cross. She explained she had already turned two people away to whom she could have let our room. My response was less than polite. I appreciated we had let her down, but finances were not uppermost in my mind as we stood, cold, wet and exhausted, in the fading light on the top of a mountain, going backwards! We pressed on. Somewhere, buried deep in a saddlebag, lay a hip flask of brandy. It's not called a hip flask for nothing. After day one we made very sure it was the most readily accessible item of equipment.

At some point Nan dropped her whip. 'Bugger,' she said. 'Shit!' We watched it sinking into the mud. 'Sod the thing,' she decided. 'Leave it there, I can't face getting off again.' It is a measure of how beaten we felt that we rode off and left it there.

We trotted most of the way back to the village, but lost the race against the dark. There were no birds to divert our attention from our aching bits and pieces. 'Bats!' cried Nan. If you are out riding and you see bats you know things have not gone according to plan. Somewhere in the packs, no doubt snuggled up to the hip flask, were our reflective strips and headlamp. The idea of stopping to dig for them was never even mooted. We trusted to the horses' white markings and the sparks coming from Sooty's shoes.

We reached Aber Farm, the home of Jane Morgan, a friend of Nan's, who did B&B. She had no vacant rooms, but took one look at us and recognised desperation and exhaustion. Nan dismounted and we followed Jane to a loose-barn in a small paddock. Jane magically produced two filled haynets. Nan looked up at me. 'You'll have to get off now!' she said. I think I could have slept where I was.

We left the horses and Jane drove us to the White Hart in Talybont. Mercifully, they had a room. As we entered the bar carrying our saddlebags and still wearing our riding hats all we could think of was a stiff drink and a bath.

'Have you been riding?' a drinker asked.

'No, we always dress up like this to go out on a Saturday night,' I spat at him. Another important commodity for this kind of escapade is a plentiful supply of patience. This was day one, and mine was already running low. I bought some cigarettes and then asked for a box of matches. When the barman handed me a packet of pork scratchings I began to think I'd really lost the plot. Nan had to reassure me for days afterwards that it was his hearing that was the problem, and that I had not been speaking gibberish.

Later, as we lay on our comfy beds, blissfully numbed by wine, I did some calculations. We had ridden 23 miles and ended up six miles from the point where we started. We were both worn out, the horses must have been stiff, too, we hadn't eaten properly, we'd failed to reach our first destination and we hadn't had a sensible conversation with anybody. Weeks of this lay ahead. What on earth had I let us in for?

Day Two – The Brecon Beacons

After a full English breakfast we returned to the horses the next day. We felt a little guilty that we had eaten so well and they had had to make do with a bit of hay and some meagre pickings of grass. They seemed quite pleased to see us, which could have had something to do with the carrots we gave them, or their misguided belief that we would take them home. We tacked up under warm sunshine, trying new configurations and knots in an attempt to avoid shifting packs. We continued along the lane through Pencelli, where we made our first pub stop. It was a little early in the day, but things kept falling off despite our best efforts, so further adjustments were needed. Two small children appeared and we let them sit on the horses, which appeared to enjoy the attention. The girls later struggled back with buckets of water which, rather embarrassingly, neither Sooty nor Holly would drink.

A few miles further on and my Barbour dropped to the tarmac yet again. At the same moment we saw a tall, strange figure striding towards us. From beneath a floppy sunhat, dark wavy hair hung down past his shoulders. Here an impressive beard took up the line. As he drew closer Nan and I exchanged glances, 'Dave!' He squinted at us for a moment before recognition dawned. It was odd to bump into someone we both knew but hadn't seen for nearly ten years. We stood there in the middle of the road, trying to explain what we were doing and to catch up on the missing decade. Apart from the beard being a little more grizzled he hadn't changed at all. He still lived in the same house, still ran his own graphics business and was still The Grateful Dead's number one fan. I marvelled at the consistency of his life and decided not to trouble him with the chaotic nature of my own. Was it because he lived in Brecon that he was able to maintain such stability, such peace? Or was it his nature? Perhaps he would have been the same in London. I doubt it though. I still can't decide if I envy him his calm and steadiness or if the thought of his unchanging existence panics me. At least he picked up my coat for me.

We twisted along leafy lanes through the picturesque village of Llanfrynach. The Beacons rear up behind it, yet it feels strangely English. Manicured. Tidy. The route we followed took us through old parkland, home to magnificent ancient oaks, Scots pines and Wellingtonia. We headed up through Libanus towards the visitors' centre on Mynydd Illtyd. This is an ideal spot for anyone wishing to walk on a gentler part of the Beacons as you can drive up to the centre on its plateau. The little restaurant serves a fair range of snacks, lunches and teas, and the information centre tells you all you need to know about the surrounding mountains. The views are lovely, particularly of Pen-y-Fan, the highest of the Beacons.

Pen-y-Fan, highest of the Brecon Beacons

We knew there were hitching posts near the café so that we could safely tie up the horses and enjoy our lunch in the sunshine. What we hadn't realised was that the centre was holding an Open Weekend. We arrived to find enough vehicles to fill a supermarket car park and hundreds of people. We fought our way through the cars, admiring the way Sooty and Holly ignored the jamboree as if it were something they saw every day. We were directed to the hitching posts, but as the local abseiling club had beaten us to it and erected a tower in front of them they were of no use to us. However stoic, we couldn't expect the horses to stand for an hour in a spot where people would keep dropping out of the sky practically on to their heads. We found a hedge behind a marquee and hoped that the large bank of grass under their noses would distract them from the commotion. It did. They stuffed themselves, leaving the area neatly strimmed, and then dozed whilst Nan and I dined on ostrich burger. Well, what else would you expect to eat on the top of a Welsh mountain?

Most of the visitors seemed to be on a day out from the valleys judging by their accents. A few assumed the horses were part of the attractions and made lots of fuss of them. Sooty quite liked it. Holly didn't bother to wake up from her snooze. One family asked where we'd got them from and if they could have some too.

The four of us replete and rested and a phone call or two made, we set off again. It was lovely to be on top of open mountain. There is a Roman road crossing the flat summit with one lonely little farmhouse halfway across. Just before we moved off the road on to the springy hill grass a car stopped and the driver wound down his window, beckoning to us.

'You know there's a vicious stallion loose up here, don't you?' he asked.

We replied that we didn't, and asked what exactly he meant by 'vicious'. After some rather vague answers it turned out that this stallion was in the habit of sinking his teeth into riders' legs in an attempt to pull them off so that he could mount the mares. The reason the man knew all this was that this dangerous creature belonged to him. We weren't sure whether to thank him for the warning or berate him for letting such an animal loose on an unsuspecting public. He sped off before we had a chance to do either. We scanned the horizon but could see only sheep and peewits. I enjoy watching peewits and listening to their distinctive cries, but didn't think this was a good time to hang about. 'Let's try and find third gear,' Nan suggested.

Now this really was going to put our packs to the test. We aimed the horses at a gentle grassy incline and searched for the cantilever. After a moment's hesitation they both fell into a fabulous, rolling canter, eating up the ground, saddlebags flapping and bumping, warm air blowing away flies, cobwebs and any tiredness. When we eventually came to a breathless halt some time later we all felt refreshed and happy. Much to our amazement we still had all our equipment. We paused to catch our breath and gaze at the small lake a little way to our left.

There is a wonderful Welsh legend regarding the Lady of the Lake. It tells the story of a young farmer who one day saw an exquisitely beautiful woman walking out of a lake. He fell deeply and incurably in love with her and begged her to marry him. She refused, saying she knew the ways of men and that it would be an impossible match. He persisted, promising he would love here always and treat her with the greatest care and kindness. Eventually, because she too was in love, she capitulated, and agreed to become his wife. She warned him, however, that if he struck her three times she would return to the lake and he would lose her forever. Naturally he swore he would never raise his hand to her.

For many years they lived happily together and had three sons. One day he unthinkingly tapped her on the shoulder for forgetting to mend his shirt. Sadness clouded her face and she reminded him of her warning, saying that now he had struck the first blow. Sometime later, whilst sharing an amusing story with his wife, he playfully slapped her on the back. Tears came to her eyes and he realised he had broken his promise a second time. Meanwhile the children grew into fine boys and the love between the happy couple was as strong as ever, but she carried with her a melancholy born of the conviction that their time together was limited. Sure enough, one day he affectionately patted her cheek. With a look that broke his heart but without a single word his wife turned away and went back into the lake. He was grief-stricken but knew he would never see her again and refused to go near the lake. Her sons could not come to terms with the loss of their mother, however, and went every day to stand at the water's edge calling to her. They were lonely and lost, and angry that she had left them to face life without her. One day she answered their calls and briefly emerged from the lake to give them a bundle before disappearing beneath the surface again. The bundle contained the healing secrets from the Otherworld, and her sons became the physicians of Myddfai. Their wisdom was passed to their descendants who practised healing for many years.

Nan and I began our descent from Mynydd Illtyd, following meandering, single-track roads down towards the valley. We passed a middle-aged farmer leaning against his Land Rover. The road went through his farm. His barns were spread on either side, and were mostly in a poor state of repair. He didn't return our greetings but after a while observed, 'It must be nice to have a horse.' There was something about the way he said it. The words themselves were harmless enough, but his tone was acid, loaded with all manner of dark criticism and judgement. In the past I have encountered attitudes of prejudice and even hostility while riding. Possibly this has its roots in class issues, stereotypical ideas of people who ride, or, more simply, envy. Some people refuse to let go of the fallacy that horse riding is an elitist sport. In every lowly hacker they see the polo player, the race-horse owner and the Master of Foxhounds rolled into one. I can, if I'm feeling generous, forgive this of city-dwellers who may have no idea of country life; or people who are having a difficult time and can't stand seeing others enjoying themselves. But we were riding worka-day horses that, as a pair, were not worth half this farmer's Land Rover. These were the very type of animal his grandfather probably used to gather his sheep from the hill. We had greeted him openly and with a genuine respect for his way of life. What was it that made him despise us on sight? I wanted to ask him, but thought better of it, but-toned my beak, and rode on.

The lane twisted through several little farms, often passing through their yards. One had an impressive collection of fowl. Two rather shy peacocks hid behind a tractor, some placid geese filed past us to a pond. Furry-footed bantams darted hither and thither. Half a dozen guinea fowl (or gleanies, as they are known locally) hummed and hawed about which way to flee before losing interest in doing anything and just watching us go by.

The next farm was far less welcoming. As we approached a pack of five sheepdogs ran barking and snarling towards us. The horses are quite used to dogs and initially took no notice, but these boys meant business. They circled us, snapping at Holly's heels, baring their teeth and lunging at us. We shouted at them, using common terms for controlling working collies such as 'That'll do!' or 'Lie down!' but they took no notice. Apart from which we could hardly make our-selves heard above all the barking and growling. Nan resorted to swearing at them, but they just swore back. At one point a particu-larly vicious dog climbed a bale, the better to launch itself at Nan's leg. Thankfully it misjudged the distance and dropped to the tarmac. Holly was becoming frightened, shooting forwards, rolling her eyes and snorting. She showed no signs of kicking them, though I rather wished she would. It was an unnerving experience. What really an-noyed me was that no one appeared to call the dogs off. There were cars parked by the farmhouse, and the commotion could be heard across the valley. Responsible dog ownership this was not. I can only hope that it was the sight of the horses that inflamed them. If not, had we been on foot, we would certainly have been bitten.

We reached the village of Abercamlais and headed for the house of an old friend of mine, Nikki, who had found us a field for the horses for the night. Nikki is a riding instructor and a keen and successful

Arab-racing jockey. She has always had a bottomless supply of energy and still finds time to race and teach whilst bringing up two small children, running a home for retired horses and maintaining a successful marriage to her lovely Dutch husband, Raymond. She greeted us with a glass of wine in her hand. 'Hi! You made it! Let's put the horses in the paddock and then you can come and join the party. We've got friends over from Holland and others coming to celebrate a birthday.'

The horses' faces visibly brightened when they saw the shady, grassy place they were to stay. We untacked and they wandered off happily to graze. Nan and I were feeling very stiff. We both had sheepskin covers on our saddles, but still had difficulty sitting down. Our legs already seemed to have forgotten how to work properly when walking. Nan had whiplash problems from Sooty's frequent attempts to snatch a mouthful of grass from the hedgerows, and I had developed an aching shoulder after twisting awkwardly to readjust a saddlebag. We hobbled to the large table in the garden and Raymond welcomed us through plumes of smoke from the barbecue. Children ran round squealing in two different languages. We lowered ourselves gingerly on to wooden benches. Our hosts looked after us very well with a constant supply of wine and food and lively conversation. The party of about fifteen comprised mostly Dutch and English with the odd Welsh person in there somewhere.

The Dutch visitors spoke of the charm and dramatic beauty of the place, but naturally complained about the weather. The English explained how they had escaped from England but now seemed to be working harder than ever. And the Welsh shrugged and said however many times they tried to leave they always ended up coming back.

Nikki's sister had broken free of her London existence and now lived but a short trot from the Visitors' Centre we had just come from. She runs a graphic design business from her new home. It was going well, but she was rather more concerned with her snail problem. A keen gardener, she was plagued by the things. She had never encountered them in such numbers before and searched for the source. She did not have far to look. Her neighbour, a former rock star, had also headed for the hills in search of tranquillity and a more natural existence. Needing a pastime that might provide a small income to supplement dwindling record royalties he had struck upon the idea of a snail farm. Perhaps snails represented the pace of life he craved. All went well until the gastropods developed some sort of illness. Seeing their relatives shrivel up, the rest of the herd(?) fled into the neighbouring garden. Where they are now very happy, thank you very much, and resist all attempts to be evicted. Who says life in the city is more stressful?

Finding himself in the Welsh mountains after a business life in Holland, Raymond had shown great initiative in starting up a Land Rover safari business. For several years he had taken people high up into the Beacons in 4-wheel drive vehicles, helping them access some of the most spectacular areas of the mountains. He has a natural charm and enthusiasm that would surely have made it an enjoyable experience for his clients. The many forms of business that make up the tourist industry in Wales are testament to people's ingenuity, and the lack of alternative viable employment (see snails above).

Nikki's friend Megan owns a neat, spacious hotel two miles up the road where we were found a billet. We felt a little self-conscious tramping through the rather elegant lounge still in our riding clothes and carrying our saddlebags like a couple of Jane Waynes. They are probably still trying to get the horsehair out of the carpet.

At least we had made some progress on our route and were beginning to feel that maybe the whole thing wasn't such a bad idea after all.

Day Three – Rescued

When the alarm clock rang the next morning neither of us had the energy to switch it off. Eventually Nan spoke. 'Can you move?' she asked.

'Not without extreme pain.'

We began to giggle. 'Oh, God!' she said. 'It's only day three and we're knackered.'

'It'll get better,' I promised. 'Our bodies will get used to it. If they don't seize up completely first.'

It was half an hour before we could struggle into a sitting position. We studied the weather forecast on the TV. It was not good: heavy rain and strong winds. I pulled out a map and checked the route.

'Well,' I said, 'we have a choice. Twelve miles, over the top of the Black Mountain where we will be completely exposed to the worst of the weather, or eighteen miles at lower altitudes but involving the A40.'

Nan winced. It wasn't really a choice. Neither of us would seriously contemplate any distance on the A40 if there were an alternative.

'There's a Roman camp on top of the mountain. We'd pass right by it.' I offered this by way of enticement. Nan thought about it as she gulped her tea.

'Do we actually have anywhere to stay at the end of today's ride?' she asked, not unreasonably.

'Not exactly. That is, not yet, no. But I'll look in the Yellow Pages, make a few phone calls. Don't worry.'

There was a pause as she finished her tea. 'Mountain,' she said. 'Definitely mountain.'

'Right. Mountain it is.'

We feasted on an enormous breakfast, which seemed a sensible move as our route was depressingly devoid of pubs. I made several fruitless phone calls before being given the number of the Lluest Trust Rescue Centre for Horses. Iean listened to my request and explanation of what we were trying to do.

'You'd better come to us,' he said. 'I think that'd be best. We have stables for the horses. You're very welcome to stay here yourselves too.'

Lluest is clearly not called a rescue centre for nothing. As it turned out, we were also invited to spend the night with some old friends of Nan's near Llandeilo. So it was arranged. The horses would stay at Lluest, and we would visit Ivor and Jane.

We prepared ourselves for what we knew would be a difficult ride. Nan wore her floor-length Dryz-a-bone, whilst I donned Barbour and very glamorous waterproof leggings. We rustled through the hotel and Megan kindly drove us back to the horses. The light drizzle gave no real indication of the atrocious weather we were to encounter later in the day.

It always amazed us how readily the horses came to us each morning. They could have been forgiven for fleeing, desperate to avoid further gruelling treks into the unknown. But again they came to us happily, accepted the offered carrots and stood quietly while we tacked and packed. We added muesli bars and wine to our supplies to see us through the day.

The first few miles were straightforward enough. We took the back roads round Dyfynnog, trotting whenever possible to cover the dis-

Twin room at the Lluest Trust

tance. We went through the daily routine of selecting a suitable stick for Nan from the hedge, since her whip still languished on top of Cantref Mountain. It wasn't that she really needed to use it on Sooty, he just seemed to jib at things less if she were carrying it, and it was always useful to ward off dogs.

We were leaving the Brecon Beacons behind us now and heading for the Black Mountain, which is actually part of a range. Both areas are dramatic and rugged, enclosed only to a certain height and then wild and open on top. In good weather they look safe enough, but there are sharp drops and bogs to catch the unwary, and it's easy to get lost. A map and a good compass are essential if you are planning to strike off from the few roads which cross the mountains. When riding it's important to appreciate how uneven the surface is, especially if your horse is not used to the area. What appears to be a grassy expanse can often be made up of tussocks, thinly covered rocks, rabbit holes or bog. It's tempting to gallop across the wide green swathes, but without a guide it's safer to stick to well-used paths or sheep tracks. There are bridle paths marked on maps, but sadly many are blocked and they are not easy to find. On private land you may discover they are not marked at all or have gates which cannot be opened. On open hill it's difficult to tell one track from another.

We fortified ourselves with snacks and some wine before the ascent up to the pine forests and the hill. The rain was now heavy and being driven at us by a strong wind. The higher we went, the grimmer it became. Despite the relative shelter afforded by the pine plantations, the rain was still being driven down our necks and into our boots. The noise was such that we had to yell at each other to be heard at all. At one point the silk blew off my hat.

'Stop!' I screamed at Nan. She heard me the third time. Getting off was an unattractive idea as it was raining so hard that my sheepskin saddle cover would be soaked by the time I got back on again. Waterproof trousers or no, I didn't want to risk a damp bum for the next eight miles. I manoeuvred Holly as close to the soggy silk as I could. Leaning forward I was able to hook it onto the end of my whip. I lifted it up in triumph and quickly stuffed it into my pocket before it had a chance to blow away again. Without any sort of peak the rain now ran down my face as if I were under a power shower. Thank God for waterproof mascara!

Sooty and Nan scored extra points for opening the next gate without her having to dismount. Now we were out of the trees and on top of the hill. Low cloud had settled around us so that visibility was reduced to less than five yards. The wind was alarmingly strong. We decided the only thing to do was to keep trotting so as to get off the mountain and down into the shelter of the lanes as quickly as possible. Every time we rose to the trot the wind pushed us back. The horses put their heads down, turned their ears in an attempt to keep the water out, and pushed on. It seemed endless. We couldn't see the spectacular scenery that we knew surrounded us. We could barely see each other. Even the sheep had taken cover. I could feel the rain working its way through my layers of clothing and had to keep spitting water out of my mouth and nose. The horses were wonderful. They didn't shy or need urging on, though they must have been hating the conditions as much as we were. I can only think that they had enough trust in us to believe we would get them out of this if they did as we told them. Never mind that we'd got them into it in the first place!

I pulled the map out of my pocket and squinted at it. Judging by the time we'd been trotting since leaving the trees I could work out roughly where we were. We still had at least another 30 minutes along the top of the hill before we could start descending.

'Roman camp!' I bellowed, pointing into the white-out on my left.

'Oh, lovely!' Nan yelled back. 'How much more of this?'

'Oh, not far.'

'What?'

'Not far!' I screamed, thankful she couldn't see the disintegrating doily that had been the map. I stuffed its remains in my pocket, hoping I'd be able to navigate the rest of the day's journey without it.

Our muscles were aching from the amount of trotting and I could feel the dampness and cold beginning to make them stiffen. The thickening cloud was eerie and disorienting. The force of the rain stung my face. And this was August! I made a note never to visit this place in winter. And yet still the horses didn't dawdle or complain or slow up.

The Celts didn't use horses as draught animals, considering them too noble and important. To them the horse symbolised power, fertility, speed and sometimes death. Rhiannon, Queen of the Otherworld, rode a white horse. Although she would ride her mount at a walk, mortals could gallop for days but never catch up with her. Her heart was won by Pwyll, Prince of Dyfed, however, and they did eventually marry. But a match between a goddess and a mortal could only cause trouble, and she was to undergo humiliation as a punishment for lowering herself from her true position. Later, when she gave birth to

twins, her daughter was human but her son was a colt. The Celts re-
lied heavily upon strong, fast horses in battle, and the reverence they
showed them is illustrated by their important position in Celtic mythology.

At last we reached another gate, we had crossed the mountain. A
mile or two along lanes brought us to a village shop. I held the horses,
the relentless rain still drenching us, whilst Nan hammered on the
door demanding chocolate.

'Sugar hit,' she said, handing me a couple of bars. We ate them in
silent relief, giving the horses a chunk or two as a small reward. The
lanes twisted downwards and the surfaces were steep and slippery.
We walked now, all too tired to go any faster. My map was unreadable
and I had never been in this area before. From my memories of studying the doily in its previous existence as a map I knew we had to make
a couple of left turns and a couple of right turns, but I wasn't sure in
which order, and there were no signposts to help. Somebody must
have been guiding us because after an hour of instinctive navigation
and not a single bum steer we arrived at Belli-Berw, the home of the
Lluest Trust.

The small farm was immaculate, with white-painted railed fences,
mowed lawns, whitewashed barns and stables and properly hung
gates. Several elderly but obviously well cared for ponies made their
way across the fields to study the new arrivals. Linda and Iean welcomed us warmly, helping us with our packs and leading the horses
into two beautiful stables inside a lovely, old stone barn. The beds
were deep and comfy and the haynets filled and sweet smelling.

We must have looked fairly pathetic. 'Well,' observed Iean, 'you
couldn't have picked a worse day.' We agreed. 'Yes,' he repeated,
watching us shake the water from our hats, 'you couldn't have picked
a worse day.'

He was a small, wiry man, about the same height as his smiley
wife. They both sported sweatshirts emblazoned with the Lluest
Trust emblem. They took a flattering interest in the horses, enquiring
after their breed and history. They patted them and studied them
with genuine interest. After some time, reluctant to tear themselves
away from Sooty and Holly, they invited us in for coffee. We accepted
gratefully. While we waited for Jane to come and collect us we asked
them about the trust. It had been founded by a young woman named
Ginny whose love of horses had compelled her to collect all manner
of desperate equines. She raised money however she could and devoted her time to rescuing the ill-treated, old, neglected and un-

wanted, and giving them a knowledgeable, caring home. Sadly, she had been stricken by cancer, and, after a long struggle, died at the age of 38. She left a grieving husband and a wide circle of admiring friends who were determined to maintain the place as she would have wanted. Her legacy is a sanctuary that is open to all and any horses that need it. Linda and Iean live and work there full-time now, travelling the country to save horses and restore them to health. Some go to new homes, but many live out the remainder of their lives in comfort and security at Belli-Berw. Ginny is buried on the farm, and her presence is very obvious.

Iean had been a miner for many years before being made redundant. I asked him about the contrast between spending all day underground and working, as he did now, out in all weathers, devoting his energies to the horses. He told me how he loved both lives. For him life in the pits had not been about danger, darkness and back-breaking work, but about the people he had worked with, the strong bond between the miners and the sense of purpose they shared. He had been sad to leave but now he enjoyed being with the horses, watching frightened, broken animals recover and thrive. He enjoyed working with his wife and making Lluest their life by taking up where Ginny had left off. He still found time to say at least three more times that we couldn't have picked a worse day for crossing the Black Mountain.

'It picked us,' Nan explained.

By the time Jane arrived to pick us up we were both cold and aching. We kissed the horses goodnight, hoping that Sooty would settle. This could quite possibly have been his first night in a stable, and he was restless, but we knew they were in the best possible hands.

Jane and Ivor live in a dear little cottage in the village of Carmel, close to Llandeilo. They share their home with four dogs, two cats and numerous tropical frogs. Jane is a garden historian under contract to Cadw: Welsh Historic Monuments. Ivor is the Director of Horticulture at the National Botanical Garden of Wales. This is an ambitious project being executed as part of the millennium celebrations. Working closely with the main universities, its aim is to provide a central botanical garden for Wales that will have a truly global aspect. Plants are being collected from all over the world. Half the finances are coming from the Millennium Fund, the rest are being provided by the Welsh Development Agency, Welsh Tourist Board and EEC grants. In all there are 568 acres, and while it is under construction over one hundred people are employed in its development. When completed there will be a staff of nearly eighty, plus 'spin-off' work and trade for about 120. There is a strong commitment to education, with school visits already happening, the better to explain organic gardening, botany and broader issues of conservation and plant life from all continents. Ivor is clearly very committed to and excited about the project and fairly confident it will be ready for its opening in July 2000.

As dusk fell Ivor invited me to join him in feeding the frogs. When Jane warned me this involved sucking flies off plants in the garden I thought better of it. Each to his own.

Nan and I enjoyed hot baths and a lovely meal in good company. So far, with the odd exception, we had been helped by people we knew. As we rode further west, however, our connections would dwindle and we would have to rely more on total strangers. As I drifted off to sleep in a blissfully soft bed I thought of the horses, comfy and dry in their warm stables. I hoped their luxury accommodation would go some way towards making up for the unpleasant day's work we had put them through. It was probably just as well that at the time I was unaware that this was indeed only Sooty's second night in a stable. Later Angela told me the only time she had shut him in a box he had panicked and jumped out through the window, landing on his back on the concrete. I fell asleep, happily unaware of his stabling history, and very glad to hear that the next day's weather promised to be warm, dry and sunny.

Day Four – Be mindful of the now

We started the morning with a spot of shopping in Llandeilo. This is a busy little town approached via a curving bridge which spans the Teifi. We bought carrots for the horses, snacks for our packs and postcards for family. Spotting a sports shop, Nan suggested we go in and see if we could buy her a new whip.

Inside, the proprietor was chatting to a customer in Welsh as he examined some fishing rods. After a while she turned to us.

'Have you got any whips?' Nan asked.

She replied in a frantic stream of Welsh, the only word of which we understood was 'kinky!' In English she added, 'You'll have to go to Carmarthen for that sort of thing!'

Maybe it was the sight of Nan's spurs that did it. We hurried out of the shop. Jane assured us that news of the two perverted English women would be round the town by lunchtime.

Back at Lluest we found the horses fit and well. They ate the carrots more out of politeness than anything else as they had already been given a special little breakfast and some apples. As we tacked up I noticed the saddlebags were beginning to rub bald patches on Holly's back. I adjusted the load slightly to vary the weight distribution, but realised that this was something that would have to be watched if she wasn't to get sore. They both walked out of their stables a little stiffly, but perfectly sound. We were waved off by an assortment of dogs, cats, a tame lamb and Iean and Linda, who seemed quite sad to part with Holly and Sooty. Anyone wishing to find out more about the Lluest Trust or make a donation will find details in the address list at the back of this book.

We had planned a fairly short ride after the demands of the previous day. I was to stay at the Plas Taliaris Meditation Centre, and Nan would be collected for another evening with Jane. After a few phone calls arrangements were made for the horses in a field at Taliaris. We walked the first mile or so to gently work the stiffness out of the horses. We followed the river north-west in a deep, narrow valley. The sunshine made everything so much easier and more enjoyable. We had been told to look out for red kites. Neither Nan nor I had ever seen one and we kept peering at distant buzzards and wondering. Jane assured us we'd know one when we saw it.

We had a short piece of main road to negotiate before we would reach Llangadog. The horses were amazingly calm in traffic. In fact, it bothered Nan and I more than it did them. Every now and again we would shout out 'Lorry! Lorry!' but the horses took not the slightest notice. Just to be on the safe side, we always put Holly in front on busy roads and through towns. She might snort at things and hesitate sometimes, and her natural pace was a little slower than Sooty's, but we couldn't risk his occasional sideways leaps. He never bothered if he was behind, leaving it to Holly to let him know if there was anything worth panicking about. Most drivers gave us a fairly wide berth and reduced their speed. One or two, however, forced their way past us without crossing the white line, practically under our stirrups.

We tackled a prime selection of hazards in Llangadog. It's a large village rather than a small town, but don't get any ideas of gorgeous cottages and delightful gardens. We saw two pubs (shut), one shop (open) and several large, noisy factories. The biggest of these turned out to be a place for producing cream. Its modern, metallic structure banished forever all images of wooden churns and dairymaids. I later discovered that this area is known as 'The Milky Way'. Apparently the cream content of the milk is higher than that produced anywhere else in the country. The pastures in the river valley certainly looked verdant and nutritious, but whoever heard of Carmarthenshire cream? I suppose it goes into branded pots of various kinds and its origins remain a secret.

We scuttled across the A40 at a junction and rode uphill. Looking back we could see the mountain we had snorkelled over the day before. Now it stood gleaming in the sunshine, looking like a Sunday afternoon stroll.

'The views from up there must be amazing,' I said.

'We will never know,' Nan quipped. 'I bet if we headed up there right now it would start raining again.'

We found a gate to tie the horses to so that they could have a rest while we ate our lunch. No sooner had we got our small loops of baler-twine out (of which, more later) than a rowdy herd of cattle appeared, gambolling up to the gate. They meant no harm, but neither Sooty nor Holly wanted to stand nose to wet nose with this boisterous bunch. Added to which they brought with them swarms of flies, many of the biting variety, and seemed to have a complete absence of bowel control. We moved the horses to another gate.

Back to the string loops. It is prudent to tie the horses' ropes to baler-twine, which is, in turn, attached to the gate. This means that if something seriously frightens the horse it will break the string rather than its neck. Of course, it doesn't solve the problem of feeble gates. I once witnessed a horse lean back, remove gate and post and disappear, clattering up the road, ploughing the tarmac as it went.

Nan and I enjoyed a quick roll in the hedge. A cheese roll that is. We gazed at the Black Mountain, wondering what other tests lay ahead. A car drew up in front of us. A man with a broad Scottish accent got out.

'Can you tell me the way to the water treatment works?' he asked.

'We haven't passed it,' I replied.

I'm sure he thought we were being deliberately unhelpful. 'I've been driving round these lanes for hours,' he explained.

'Well, it's not that way,' I said, pointing back the way we'd come. 'As for that way,' I waved my roll up the road, 'I'm afraid I can't help you. I have no idea what's round the next corner.'

He ran a sweaty palm through his thinning hair. 'But you're riding.' He pointed at the horses as if we might not have noticed them. 'You must be local.'

'Sorry,' said Nan. 'We've come from Crickhowell. We don't know this area. That is, only where we've been, not where we're going.' Crickhowell clearly meant nothing to him but he decided we were only adding to his bad day and climbed back into his car.

'Hope you find it!' I called after him. He passed us an hour later going in the opposite direction.

We'd arranged to meet Alison Mostyn, a friend of Jane's, who would take us to the farm where the horses were to stay. It was getting really quite hot and one of Nan's packs kept slipping. By the time we reached the village we were all pretty sweaty and the horses were thirsty. There was a stream nearby, but it wasn't possible to get the horses down to it.

Alison arrived with her children and Labrador, fresh from a day on the beach, which was only an hour's drive away. The children sat on the horses for a while before we untacked them. The field belonged to Gareth Davies, an open, friendly man who was happy to help. He told us about his well-known herd of Welsh Black cattle, of which he was justly proud. His stock is highly thought of by those in the know. He was a serious and successful farmer, but explained he was encouraging his sons to get a good education and gain useful qualifications. 'We can't say what the future holds for farmers.'

Alison took us home for a cup of tea and I asked her what the locals thought of the Taliaris Centre. The information I had was that the place was inhabited, owned and run by a small group of people who ran meditation workshops, weekends of alternative therapies, esoteric studies and talks. Anywhere that could be described as a commune still carries a certain stigma and some pretty entrenched ideas. I was interested to find out how the place was viewed by the people who lived in the area. She said that on the whole they were accepted. People had got used to them. They were quiet, looked after the old house and its grounds, and didn't attempt to force their own way of life upon anyone else. One part of their enterprise had caused some conflict, however. One of the members of the community owned several hundred acres of woodland and lakes. He wanted to develop it into an ecological park of sorts, erecting one or two eco-dwellings, or houses sunk into the ground. The locals had feared another 'tepee village' springing up. This was their description of a much larger community a few miles away which regularly holds festivals and gatherings, attracting large numbers of people. It is definitely not in favour with the indigenous population.

Alison kindly drove us to Plas Taliaris, where Nan was whisked off by Jane. I was warmly greeted by Jenny, who suggested the tack could stay in the hallway. She quickly explained the rule of no outdoor shoes inside the house. I removed my boots, embarrassed at the unfriendliness of my feet.

Plas Taliaris is an imposing Georgian mansion, complete with columned portico. As you stand on the steps the land falls away, a rolling vista of green stretching to the blue hills beyond. Inside, the drawing room still has splendid oak panelling and an intricately decorated stucco ceiling. I left my bags in my room, which was fresh and light. Jenny, a woman who oozed contentment, briefly showed me the kitchen, where other members of the community were busy preparing dinner, and then the meditation room. It certainly had an air of calm and serenity about it. The ceiling was high, the full length windows flooded it with natural light, and the tranquil blue colours all made me want to lie down on the wall-to-wall meditation mats and pass out. I was aching less, but still felt exhausted. It was sweet of Jenny to take the time to show me the grounds, but the very thought of an hour's walk drained me.

However, the effort was well rewarded. The walled garden was beautifully tended and full of the herbs and vegetables which fed the inhabitants of Taliaris. Everything was organically grown with great care, which clearly paid off. There was a wilderness garden, a jungle of wild flowers and aged trees.

'We like to remind people how to walk in nature,' Jenny told me, striding ahead. I fought my way through the undergrowth, fully appreciating nature, but rather feeling I'd seen quite a lot of it lately and a bath and a bit of mindless TV were very appealing.

We made our way up through the woods. I asked if there were any bridle paths. 'Not really,' said Jenny. 'There was talk of making some permanent rides through the trees, but nobody could reach agreement on where and how many so the idea was scrapped.'

The set of hoofprints we followed up the hill clearly showed that someone had made up their own mind about access. The lake at the top was charming. There was no view as it was surrounded by trees, and somehow this gave a feeling of being completely removed from the rest of the world. I could see how such a place would revive the city-weary senses of stressed-out visitors who came in search of inner peace.

By the time we returned to the house we had 15 minutes to get ready for dinner. I washed and dug out my only non-riding garment. This was a crease-proof, wraparound, long skirt. I added a clean T-shirt and hoped I didn't smell of eau d'equine. A little cat trotted into my room. Somehow one would expect some aloof, exotic animal in such a place, but Lilly was a common-or-garden fluffy tabby, and I liked her all the better for it. She followed me downstairs.

The dining room was sparsely decorated and spacious. The tables were precisely cat-height. If Lilly positioned herself comfortably in front of a plate she was at exactly the right level to eat. The rest of us had to arrange our legs in some sort of yogic position to get anywhere near the food. My skirt proved to be a bad choice for this exercise, unwrapping itself however I tried to sit. Not so bad if one was exposing a pair of nicely tanned limbs, but mine had been encased in jodhpurs and so were anaemically white, with the attractive addition of seam grooves and sock ribbings. Lovely.

Nick, a serious-looking man who gave the impression of always having something on his mind, suggested that we wait until everyone was seated and then I could tell them what I was doing and ask any questions. There were seven of us in all: John, who was in charge of the garden; Nick; Jenny; a vibrant Brazilian woman called Regina; Jenny's friend Pete; myself and Sarah, a pale, delicate woman who never smiled.

I was beginning to feel nervous. I was the outsider here, and although they were doing their best to make me feel welcome, I was aware that I didn't fit in. Maybe they were a little wary of me, knowing I was going to write about them, and this put them a little on their guard.

The food was wonderful. Most of the ingredients had come from the garden. There was a large plate of baked red and yellow tomatoes with basil, two succulent and filling nut roasts, an enormous green salad and some delicious garlic potatoes roasted in their skins. I relaxed a little when Nick asked me if I would prefer red or white wine with my meal. I had half expected a dry house.

Everyone assembled, dropping to the floor with comfortable, practised ease. Lilly helped me out by curling up on my lap, anchoring my wretched skirt.

I briefly outlined my project – riding, writing, exploring the landscape, and investigating the different ways people lived in rural Wales. They gave me their full and polite attention. I was sure I was talking too much and too loudly. I felt like Ruby Wax in a room full of Buddhist monks. I even apologised for gabbling. Sarah said it was OK, they enjoyed visitors from London as they could draw on their energy. To a man, they spoke softly and slowly, considering their words. Most of them also had the unnerving habit of fixing their gaze in the middle distance somewhere over my left shoulder when talking to me. At one point I actually turned round to see if there was some deeply fascinating picture there. Nothing. Blank wall. Somewhere near the end of what they were saying they would suddenly re-focus, looking you directly in the eye as they finished their point. They always seemed to do this just as I was putting a large forkful of food into my mouth. I drank my wine and gratefully accepted a refill.

Nick explained that the house had for some years been the residence of a particular teacher of meditation whose followers had gathered there to learn from him. Since his departure a few of the community members had stayed on and bought the house. Their workshops attracted a wide variety of visitors. Some came for dance or meditation weekends, others to hear a particular speaker or special practitioner. Recently they had held a highly successful family weekend. The concept of finding inner peace with a mob of small children racketing about was a strange one, I thought, but it had worked. Even the youngsters had entered into the spirit of the thing and accepted the 'quiet time' which was part of each day. John sheepishly admitted there was a television secreted away in an attic room, but it really hadn't been used much. On reflection, the family idea made sense.

After all, it was no good achieving some sort of serenity in solitude if you couldn't take it back with you into the hurly-burly of the real world. If your daily life included small children, how much better to show them what was possible, what you yourself were trying to achieve, particularly if it could be made fun and stimulating for them.

I asked Sarah how she would sum up what they tried to give the people who came to Taliaris. She paused for a moment, thinking before she spoke (something we could all learn, for a start), then said, 'We encourage them to be aware. We help them to be mindful of the now.'

At this point I was very glad Nan wasn't with me. I was trying to take the thing seriously and would have been incapable of doing so if I had caught her eye at that moment. I waited to see if Sarah was going to add anything. Nothing came. I nodded, not wishing to appear a complete idiot, but not entirely sure what she was talking about.

'I see,' I said. 'And, er, how do you do that, exactly?'

'Oh, many ways,' said Nick. 'It can start with little things.'

'Like switching off lights when you leave a room,' Jenny put in.

Ah, energy conservation, got that.

'And water,' Nick went on, 'we have our own natural supply here and we encourage people not to waste it but to appreciate it.'

All good, practical stuff, I thought.

'And, of course, meditation helps centre people. It can bring them to the now,' Jenny explained.

'You mean living in the present?' I ventured.

'Yes,' said Nick, 'but it's more than that. It's an awareness of the moment. People spend their lives rushing about, working, worrying about the future. It's good to slow down.'

It had clearly worked for them. 'But,' I asked, 'can a few days really make a difference? After all, this is a wonderful place to relax and rest, but what happens when people go back to the pressures and stresses of their normal existences?'

Nick nodded, 'I understand your point. Not everyone can live in a place like this. But we hope that each person takes something away with them. An insight or an attitude that can help them live richer, fuller, more centred lives. We can only show what's possible. The rest is up to them.'

This seemed a realistic approach. I think anyone who had done a little meditation or attended some sort of group workshop or gathering before would certainly gain something from spending time in such an environment. People new to the experience might need a little time to adjust. In some ways the atmosphere and the pace of the place were soothing. Something about it made me restless, though. I'm pretty sure all the tranquillity would have frustrated me after a while. Far from it rubbing off on me, I felt a strong desire to put on some loud rock music. Maybe I just had a lot of 'stuff' to deal with.

I asked how they felt they fitted in with the locals. They confessed there had been conflict over their plans for the woods, but nothing could be further from their minds than another 'tepee village' so people's fears on that score were groundless. On the contrary, they had some pretty sound ideas for caring for the woodland and using it to explore ways of living within the natural environment without damaging it. As for the house and its activities, they had received no complaints and often held open days and small parties where all the villagers were invited. Their curiosity satisfied the majority had accepted the community and left them to get on with it. Strange was OK, it seemed, as long as it was a quiet strange.

I told the story of Nan's attempt to buy a whip in Llandeilo. Some of them actually laughed. Sarah looked horrified. 'Why do you need whips and spurs?' she demanded.

I tried to explain, I really did. I told her about keeping horses straight in fast traffic; of fending off vicious stallions or packs of snarling dogs; of giving the horses a break from the thump-thump-thump on their ribs they had endured for the last ten years. Nothing cut any ice with her. I could see she had me down once and for all as a cruel user and abuser of defenceless animals.

Jenny's friend Pete, a visitor, not a resident member of the community, was the only Welshman present. His father was a dairy farmer, but Pete travelled the world as a sound engineer. His was certainly a life of contrasts – rock concerts in Japan one week, trips back to Taliaris the next. He, thankfully, was able to look you in the eye while he spoke. He was bright and quick-witted and smoked most of my cigarettes. This was fine by me, as it stopped me feeling I was single-handedly polluting the atmosphere. He told me how quotas had broken his father's heart, never having believed he would have seen the day when he would be literally pouring milk down the drain. 'You can't escape the craziness of the world by living here,' he said. 'It's everywhere.'

As we finished our meal John announced, 'I think it's time for a drink.' Great, I thought, a large brandy is just what I need.

'What'll you have, Nick?'

'Oh, I think peppermint tea tonight.'

'Paula?'

I arranged my features into a smile with some effort. 'Nothing for me thanks, I'm fine.'

Perhaps a few days' detox were really necessary to fully appreciate a visit to Plas Taliaris. I know it's a bit like cleaning the house because the cleaner is coming, but it might be easier to fall into the rhythm of the place that way.

Alternative ecology: a fly sucker

Day Five – The puppy, the donkey, and the elephant

The next morning was bright and clear. Sitting on the steps of the big house enjoying a coffee and a cigarette, I let my mind drift into the view. Nick joined me.

'It's glorious,' I said. 'You can see so far.'

'Yes,' he agreed, 'we're very lucky.'

He really meant it. I think people who come to live in a beautiful place never get over the impact of their surroundings while the ones who are born there can sometimes become immune to the beauty. I believe Nick genuinely drew inspiration from the flowing sea of green and the blue, distant hills every time he looked at them.

I made a few phone calls to people I'd never met, their numbers given to me by other people I'd never met, snatching at the flimsiest of connections to find a field and a place to stay. It was always a bit stressful. What I wanted seemed perfectly straightforward to me, but, of course, it took a while for others to grasp the idea. I'd tell them I was looking for B&B for two people and a field to put two horses in for one night, as we were riding through Wales. They'd say yes to this and yes to that and then assure us there was a pub nearby where we could get some food.

'Nearby?' I'd ask.

'Ooh, about ten minutes,' they would say.

'On foot?'

'No, in a car.'

How they imagined we were riding two horses and driving a car at the same time beat me.

Eventually I found us a B&B with its own paddock and assurances that a mini-cab could be found to take us to the local eatery. Hooray!

Nan arrived, I said my goodbyes, and Nick drove us up to the horses' field. They seemed to have spent a comfortable night with plenty of grass. Both had muddy feet from paddling in the stream. Holly's bald patches were slowly spreading. Worryingly, some old saddle sores were beginning to harden up again, too. The saddle she had was synthetic, rather than leather. This gave it the advantage of being very light, but under such relentless work it had begun to flatten, tipping me forwards slightly and causing pressure points on either side of Holly's withers. We smothered the horses in fly repellent as the day was hotting up and biting things were already being a nuisance. After years of experimenting and spending a small fortune on dozens of different fly repellents, which seemed to have precious little effect, I had resorted to making my own. I now use a simple mixture of citronella oil and water (about 1:25). It's cheap, it contains no scary chemicals, and it works.

Alison's children arrived to say goodbye, to the horses rather than us I'm sure. We felt a bit mean not giving them a ride, but it always took forever for us to get ready in the mornings and we were anxious to be off. We had a good 18 miles ahead of us. I noticed the children playing with a beautiful blue merle sheepdog. I haven't had a dog since moving to London five years ago. During that time I have often mused about what type of dog I would look for next, once I was in a position to own another. For the past three years I have been hankering for a small, blue merle Border Collie.

Gareth arrived on his tractor. The rare sun had no doubt sent hundreds of farmers into action, eager to make hay while…you know how it goes. I thanked him for letting us use his field and he steadfastly refused to take any payment.

'I was admiring your dog,' I told him. 'Blue merles like that are quite rare.'

'He's just fathered a litter of pups,' he told me. 'There are three more like him up in the barn.'

Puppies!

'Hold this,' I said, tossing Holly's reins to Nan.

'What?'

'Back in a minute,' I called over my shoulder as I followed Gareth and the children up to the barn.

Amongst the straw a small tri-coloured bitch lay cuddling her young. I knelt beside her. She showed her good nature by letting a total stranger, who reeked of citronella, come close to her pups. One of the children handed me the largest pup with the best markings. I held the snuffling little thing in the palm of my hand. He was only three days old, his eyes and ears not yet open, but I knew I had found my next dog. I told Gareth to keep him for me. He was a little taken aback, clearly thinking this soft female was making an impulse buy, but I assured him I was serious.

When I returned to the horses Nan raised her eyebrows at me.

'I'll explain later,' I said.

The lanes took us up above Taliaris, where we could see even further horizons. Sheltered paddocks quilted the landscape ahead as we left the towering mountains behind us. We saw numerous buzzards and trilling skylarks, but no red kites. The temperature had risen enough to make us strip to our skimpiest T-shirts. I still hadn't bought any suntan cream, so borrowed some of Nan's oil. She has a good tolerance to the sun and browns easily. I knew I was in danger of burning, but shopping was out for a few more days.

We were getting into a rhythm of sorts now. Travelling every day had become natural to us and also to the horses, which stepped out willingly. We trotted on flat bits of lane and up gentle slopes, whilst walking downhill. Sooty would have trotted anywhere, but Holly liked to take her descents cautiously. Any attempt to make her trot down a hill reduced her gait to a bone-jarring, pogo stick movement which was torture for both of us. Nan selected her daily stick, a nice piece of hazel with a few bits of swishy greenery. This was like waving a bar of chocolate under Holly's nose. Her will-power snapped and she quickly stripped every leaf off the thing in one go, despite Nan's colourful protestations.

We rode on for a few miles, developing a healthy thirst and appetite. Neither of us had eaten any breakfast, and we soon polished off our muesli bars. The water bottle I always carried on the front of my saddle was becoming very useful now. At about one o'clock we reached the hamlet of Llanfynydd. We tied the horses in the pub car park, a routine they were now very familiar with. An elderly man shuffled out of the pub, squinting into the sunshine.

'Are you open?' I asked.

'Do you want a drink?' he asked back.

'Well, yes please. A coke and a white wine with soda, if that's OK. Do you do any food?' I asked.

'I've got some crisps,' he informed us proudly.

Our hearts sank. Still, we had to eat something and the next pub was eight miles away.

'Crisps would be lovely.' I thanked him.

He returned after what seemed an age. Nan rescued the drinks from him and passed him some money. He grinned at us revealing two lovely teeth, all the more splendid for their rarity.

'Enjoy your drinks,' he said, tottering back inside and locking the door.

Nan had developed a nagging headache and the warm

Liebfraumilch and lack of food didn't improve it. There was a charming water pump next to the chapel beside the pub, but it had long since given up producing water. We would have to try and find somewhere for the horses to drink soon.

We set off again. I could feel the sun beginning to burn my left shoulder, arm and side of my face. There was little I could do to avoid it, short of riding backwards. Nan had by now stripped down to her crop top – something between a bra and a T-shirt. After all, we had passed only one car in the last seven miles or so. Of course, around the next corner we found a farmer standing in his yard by the road.

'That's a lovely sight,' he said, smiling at Nan's cleavage.

We took advantage of his attention and asked for water for the horses. He carefully filled a bucket for them, thinking they might prefer fresh water to that in the trough. Needless to say, Sooty and Holly ignored the bucket and made straight for the trough. He told us in his younger days (he couldn't have been forty) he had been a keen point-to-pointer and bred horses. Now he was too busy running his farm. A deafening noise heralded the arrival of his young son on a quad bike. Many farmers use them instead of horses now, to move stock and get about their farms. We asked if his son rode too.

'Wouldn't let him near a horse!' he exclaimed. 'My parents spent too much time visiting me in hospital. He's safer on the bike.'

Thanking him for the water and his good wishes for our trek, we moved on. We were down in the valley again now, following the river north-west towards the Brechfa forest. Nan's headache was getting worse, as was my sunburn. I checked the map. 'A couple more miles to the next village,' I told Nan. 'We should be able to find some food there.'

In fact, it was nearly four o'clock by the time we reached Brechfa. We turned into the first pub we found which declared itself open. Leaving the horses in the shade with their girths loosened, we were able to sit inside the small restaurant in comfort. We felt scruffy and dirty in such a clean and pretty room, but the landlady didn't seem to mind, nor think it strange that we wanted sandwiches in the middle of the afternoon. Returning from the loo I found Nan had gone. Through the window I could see her trying to do something to Sooty's pack, which, on closer inspection, I realised was underneath him. He had shaken and the whole lot had swung round 180 degrees. Nan spotted him peering through his front legs trying to work out what had happened. It's at times like this that a horse's calm disposition is beyond price. Most horses would have a fit if they suddenly found themselves wearing 35lbs of tack and pack Cossack-style. It took both of us to free him from his predicament. I led Nan back into the shade and fed her Disprin and ham sandwiches. A quick visit to the village shop provided us with chocolate and more cigarettes. After an hour's rest we decided to press on, still having six or seven miles to go.

We followed the lane around the edge of the Brechfa Forest. It was tempting to venture into its shady depths, but we had been warned that inside there was a maze of forestry tracks and the only actual bridle path was blocked. Getting lost in the woods for a couple of hours was all Nan needed. I tried singing to her and the horses at one point. Well, it worked for Roy Rogers. We managed two rounds of Oh, Sir Jasper, Do Not Touch Me! and a couple of You'll Never Get to Heaven. Sooty and Holly twitched their ears a lot, but gave no other indication of their reaction to being serenaded. Nan finally asked me if I were bored. I said that I wasn't, I was simply trying to raise the troops' morale. She replied morale was just fine and would be even better given some peace, quiet and really strong painkillers. I suppose singing at someone with a headache was a pretty dim idea.

The horses were noticeably tiring by the time we reached the village of Llanpumsaint. Ffwrm-y-Felin, the old mill, proved difficult to find, and when we did eventually reach it we were horrified to see its driveway blocked by a snarling cattle-grid, beside which was a very narrow gate.

'We're looking for Mrs Ryder-Owen,' I called to the teenage lad across the grid.

'I'm her son. We've been expecting you.' He opened the little gate.

'It looks a bit of a tight squeeze,' I said, thinking of our fairly broad horses and their even wider packs.

'Perhaps we should...'

'Stuff it!' Nan declared, urging Sooty on. He shot through the posts with half an inch to spare either side. Holly and I followed rather more cautiously. We untacked, dumping our packs on what we later discovered to be an ants' nest. It was one of those days, really. A small girl appeared. She must have been about six years old and came up to Holly's elbow. She had flimsy sandals on and I worried about her tiny feet so close to Holly's large, iron-clad ones. Weariness and hunger had made the animals fidgety.

'Be careful,' I warned. 'Don't stand too close.'

'It's all right, I'm used to horses,' she explained. 'Especially brown ones.'

Getting the horses to the paddock involved leading them through the garden, around the back of the house, past two lines of billowing washing, and over a footbridge. The horses were far too tired to object to any of these horrors. They both have promising future careers as police horses. There was a donkey in the field, but it didn't seem intent on causing any trouble. The horses gave him a long hard stare. Nan and I were concerned to see rather a lot of ragwort in the field. There was nothing we could do about it. Nan spoke to Sooty, pointing as she did so, 'Ragwort, donkey, grass. Eat the grass.'

Our room was delightful: clean, spacious, pretty and comfortable. I tried to organise a taxi while Nan rummaged through the packs for the first-aid kit. She joined me outside on the patio, where I was sipping some very welcome tea. We waited for the taxi. And waited. At last a car drew up. It turned out to be Mrs Ryder-Owen herself. She told us to give up on the taxi and bundled us into her car to take us to the pub.

'You don't look very well,' she said to Nan.

'I've got the grandmother of all headaches. I've had it all day.'

'Oh, you poor thing. Have you taken anything for it? I know how awful headaches can be.' Anne was, in fact, a health visitor, so she knew what she was talking about. 'I've got some Ibuprofen in the house.'

'I've just taken two,' Nan said.

'Two! Oh, make sure you drink lots of water when you get to the pub. No alcohol, mind. Poor thing. You'll feel better when you've had something to eat. I expect you're dehydrated.' She dropped us at the pub. 'Call me when you want picking up, it's no trouble.'

We thanked her and headed for the bar. Nan showed great restraint by drinking a pint of orange and lemonade before touching any wine. We ate well and began to feel human again. Very quickly the good food added to our exhaustion so that we were in danger of falling asleep, nose down in our coffees. We phoned Anne, who said she would collect us in ten minutes. The pub wasn't very busy and we chatted to the landlord and the locals while we waited. They were very friendly and more than a little surprised at our plans to ride so far. Eventually we heard a car outside. We said goodbye and were wished goodnight and good luck by the entire pub.

In the darkness of the car park we made straight for the vehicle which had just arrived. We opened the back doors and climbed in, much to the surprise of the complete stranger who was just climbing out of the driver's seat. Full of apologies, we made an embarrassing re-entry to the pub. The landlord teased the driver about how he must have thought Christmas had come early. He was definitely overestimating the appeal of two exhausted, fractious, grubby women who stank of horse and citronella. We weren't much of a prize.

When we finally found ourselves in Anne's car again I asked her what had given her the idea of doing bed and breakfast.

'Well, you see, it was because of the elephant which lives at the end of our road.'

In the back of the car Nan began to giggle in the manner of someone needing a straitjacket.

'I'm sorry.' I tried to wake up and concentrate. 'Elephant?'

Of course, there was a perfectly simple explanation. Four miles from Ffwrm-y-Felin there is a Buddhist temple. People travel great distances to visit it, especially as it has its own resident elephant. Ideal for certain ceremonies, I'm reliably informed. Often so many visitors would arrive that they could not all be accommodated. So, after a young mother and child had knocked frantically on Anne's door one night looking for a bed, she had decided it might be a good business to go into. This was her seventh year of B&B and it had proved a great success.

That night I dreamt of elephants and donkeys and deserts. Nan informs me she doesn't remember anything of the evening past taking the Ibuprofen.

The Milky Way

Day Six – Don't fence me in!

We feasted on a particularly good cooked breakfast the next morning. Nan's headache had gone, and the weather looked set fair, though not as scorching as the day before. This was a relief to me. I had some quite badly burnt patches on one shoulder and the back of my neck. As it was a little cooler I was able to cover up with a soft jumper that had been nestling at the bottom of my saddlebag. I looked a little inappropriately dressed for a summer's day, but by now that was of little importance to me. To look ridiculous for a long time, remove your hat harness from your chin after eight hours in the sun. Bikini strap marks are nothing compared with triangular white patches on your face. Nan assured me it gave the impression of high cheekbones. I was less than convinced.

The horses hadn't eaten the ragwort, which was good. Not so good was the state of Holly's digestive system after a few nights of rich grass. To those not in the know, the results are similar to those likely to afflict a human being who unaccustomedly spends two days eating vindaloo. Even less good were the donkey kisses. I didn't notice them at first, and just thought it quite sweet when Holly made friendly snuffling noises at the donkey as I led her past him. Then I noticed these strange, sticky, oval slobbers all over Holly at exactly donkey height, which was a bit of a give-away. Sooty had some, too, so heaven knows what had been going on. He looked faintly embarrassed (they can, you know). Holly was saying nothing. We just have to pray she wasn't in season, otherwise come next July...

We noticed that Sooty's off hind was beginning to wear in an unusual manner. He had a tendency to drag his back foot as he went down hill, and, presumably because of the mileage we'd done, had worn both shoe and hoof back to a straight line across the toe. If you imagine a wedge of cheese where someone has taken a greedy chunk off the thin end, you'll get an idea of what it looked like. At this point it wasn't actually causing him any problems, but the shoe would soon wear through completely and the progressive damage to the hoof would inevitably lame him if left unchecked. We would have to start looking for a farrier.

We set off in good spirits. The weather was pleasant, butterflies flitted about, I promised Nan we had no more than ten miles to travel, and we actually had a place to stay arranged. We toyed with the idea of visiting the elephant, but it would have added an extra eight miles to our day's ride.

The lanes were generally quiet apart from an unusual proliferation of yellow trucks. When the same one passed us for the third time we decided there must be some sort of gravel pit or construction site nearby.

The landscape was so different from that of a few days ago. We had crossed the dramatic expanses of the Brecon Beacons, with their steep escarpments and golden-grassed high plateaux. We had travelled over the Black Mountain, which dominated the river valley and the 'Milky Way' to its west. Now we criss-crossed the paddock-patterned low hills, all enclosed and grazed, farmed for centuries, some still with their stone walls, others with thick hedges. This was an environment tamed by man's hand and subsequently nurtured by it. In a symbiotic relationship, farmers had lived off the land whilst tending and protecting it. It was possible to view farms and soft pastures for thirty miles in all directions. The space allowed my mind to travel too, and my senses to receive the subtlest stimulation. I had only to look at the mosses on the ancient stone walls to feel their softness. Birdsong tickled my ears. The hedgerows provided an exquisite balance of colour – gentle green hazel, muted purple rosebay willowherb, creamy cow-parsley and shining yellow coltsfoot. The sweetest aroma of wild honeysuckle couldn't fail to lift the spirits. In Thomas Hardy's *Far from the Madding Crowd* Bathsheba tells Gabriel that she cannot think properly on top of the hills because her mind spreads away. But I like this feeling, and believe it gives a chance for thoughts from another plane. This is a different level of our consciousness than that which nurtures those ideas we struggle with and force in less natural, more confined surroundings.

We decided to try a bridle path. It was clearly marked on the map and would cut out a long stretch of main road. The route took us through a farmyard. A young man emerged to see who was about and said he'd only ever noticed one rider take the bridle path, and he had no idea if it was passable or not as it wasn't on his land. We pressed on. The grassy track was inviting and the horses definitely enjoyed the change of surface. We came to a gate, which Nan was determined to conquer without dismounting. She succeeded, but came away with a badly pinched finger for her efforts. We carefully took the headlands and passed through an open gateway, all the time follow-

Sooty, happy in his work

ing the line described on the map. The next corner dashed our hopes. Stretching from one side of the field to the other, directly in front of us, was a firmly planted, humming electric fence.

'Bugger!' we said in unison. We turned back, cursing farmers and moaning about the lack of success of local riders and bridleways' officers. I tackled the gate this time. Holly was co-operative, but I still managed to re-inflame my earlier shoulder injury while lifting the rusty construction. So much for bridle paths!

We were forced to ride along the very busy main road, where we encountered some of the most unnerving traffic and worst drivers so far. It was a relief to reach the village and an open pub. Sooty had developed a keenness for turning left. We think this was born of the fact that at the start of our journey the end of the day's work had been signified by turning left into their appointed paddock. He also knew a pub when he saw one. To him pubs now meant a rest and possibly a snack. I'm afraid he may still be carrying novice passengers into pub car parks they had not intended to visit.

There was nowhere to tie up the horses so I held them while Nan disappeared inside in search of refreshments. She reappeared bearing drinks and saying cheese salad sandwiches would follow. Well, they did, three-quarters of an hour later. This seemed excessively slow service, particularly as there were only four cars parked behind the pub. We availed ourselves of the boot of one of them as a picnic table, hoping the owner wouldn't appear. Naturally he did, almost at once, barely giving us time to remove our sandwiches before he sped off, bits of lettuce adorning his rear window.

Continuing on our way we eventually found the source of the yellow lorries – a large pile of gravel being moved from A to B for what I'm sure was a very good reason.

'Are you following me?' one of the drivers asked.

'We thought you were following us,' said Nan.

'Depends where you're going,' he grinned.

'Snowdonia. Race you there!' I said as we trotted off.

We had been invited to stay with Mary Baker at Clun Farm, Trelech. I had been given Mary's number by a lady named Alison, whose number I had got from Carolyn Morgan, whom I'd tracked down through the tourist information centre in Newport, Pembrokeshire. Sometimes what we were doing caught the imagination of people we had never met. So many were helpful and generous. I always felt confident that we would find a place to stay, that the horses would be safe, and that we would find help when we needed it. Maybe I was being extremely naive and we were just lucky. Maybe a positive attitude and trusting nature helped. I prefer to think it was the spontaneous friendliness of most of the people we met. They would listen to what we were trying to do and, even if they didn't understand why we were doing it, they seemed to like it. Some acted out of curiosity and many of the horsey people we met wished they were doing it themselves. For most, though, I think it was the fact that we asked for help and they were in a position to give it. How often do we get a chance to interact with strangers openly and spontaneously?

Mary keeps sheep and horses on her small farm at the edge of the village. We were offered stables, but explained that Sooty and Holly preferred to sleep out, so they were put in a gently sloping paddock behind the cottage. As had become their habit, they indulged in a rigorous bout of synchronised rolling before wandering off to graze. Nan and I took the chance to clean our tack. We had jettisoned the saddle soap before we even started the ride. Mary's kitchen was perfect for us. A glowing Rayburn aired our girths and numnahs, and there were plenty of places to hang our clean bridles and rest our gleaming saddles.

Mary admired our horses through the window. She was a knowledgeable horsewoman. Her speciality was preparing Thoroughbred yearlings for the sales, though she also had a young cob she was bringing on and an Arab she was fittening for endurance riding. Anyone who has tried knows you can't make money out of horses, so naturally, aside from the sheep, Mary had two jobs. One was milk recording, which involved getting up at an unspeakable hour to monitor local herds. She repeated the process in the evenings. She said the work had changed little in the ten years she'd been doing it, apart from the computer she was now required to use. In her spare time she worked at an alpine nursery in Trelech. As in so many parts of Britain I found it was the women who often had two part-time jobs, both fitted around running the home or tending the livestock.

My father had volunteered to take us out to supper. He lives near Llanelli, which is about a forty-minute drive from Trelech. The evening was quite cool so, having nothing clean and warm to change into, Nan and I did the best we could to tidy ourselves up but remained in jodhpurs and boots. True to form my father arrived looking disconcertingly smart with his wife, Diana, equally well turned out. He laughed at the sight of us.

'We did the best we could,' I offered lamely.

Mary had told us of the nearest place to get a good meal and we attempted to give my father directions through the labyrinthine lanes. He was a little confused when we told him to 'do a Sooty' when we meant left and 'walk on' when going straight over a crossroads. The Nag's Head was seething with campers from the local site, but we managed to find a table. There was a wide choice of good food at reasonable prices, and the portions were more than generous. The service was slow, though, and I wondered if the staff were drawn from the same pool as those who worked at the pub we had stopped at for lunch.

It was lovely to spend some time with family and relax over tasty food and good wine. It made a change not to have to explain what we were doing, where we had come from, and so on. We ate far too much, hoping Sooty and Holly wouldn't suffer from the extra weight.

That night we returned to pretty bedrooms and comfy beds in Mary's welcoming home. We felt well rested and revived and ready for what might lie ahead.

Day Seven – The Archdruid's pyjamas

Mary, Nan and I stood and stared at Sooty's foot. It really was getting worse very quickly. Only a few millimetres of iron held the shoe in one piece, and the hoof itself was a horribly unnatural shape.

'It'll need a bit of expert shoeing if you're to complete your journey,' Mary said and we agreed. We had one more day's ride to the coast, where we were due to give the horses and ourselves a day or two's rest. We would have to find a blacksmith there. We set off conscious of every step, anxiously hoping the shoe would hold out. What worried me more was the possibility that Sooty wouldn't be able to continue the trek. We had an extra horse, Timber, sitting on the substitutes' bench back at Llangenny, but we would both be sorry to break up the team. Sooty worked well with Holly, and we had become fond of him. We would have to wait and see what the farrier said.

The day was sunny, with a few small cotton-wool clouds. I wasn't the only one with sunburn. Holly's nose was in a bad way. I promised her I'd buy something for it the minute we hit civilisation.

Mary had directed us to a well-used, passable bridle path. It followed a pretty stream under willows and oaks and we all wished it were possible to spend more time 'off-piste'. But we had a long way to go and were already asking a lot of the horses. Blocked bridleways could add hours and miles to our journey, so we had to be sensible about it.

The hedgerows were glorious now. Feathery fescues grew alongside foxgloves and harebells. For once there were more butterflies than flies. Several blue ones, or cream ones with orange tipped wings alighted on the horses every now and again, hitching a ride. They appeared to quite like the citronella. Although still cultivated, the hills we were on now were higher than those of the day before, being the start of the Preseli mountain range. Sprigs of heather began to appear in the hedges, and the hills ahead were a deep purple.

We reached the village of Tegryn, which we both agreed was pretty uninspiring. It consisted almost entirely of modern houses and the ubiquitous L-shaped bungalows that never fit in anywhere. One cottage stood out as easily the most charming. It's name was Tynewydd which means 'new house', which was faintly ridiculous, it being the oldest house for five miles in any direction. We found a pub that was firmly shut. Undeterred I knocked on the door. A wary face appeared at the window.

'Any chance of a drink?' I asked.

'What sort of drink?' he wanted to know.

'Wine? A lager perhaps?' I tried.

He shook his head.

'Couldn't do that.' He thought for a minute. 'How about a can of something?'

'Yes, well, coke then, thank you.'

He handed me the warm can through the window, taking the money and studying it carefully, before disappearing. Heaven knows what he imagined we would do to him if he opened the door.

Nan found she could get a signal on her phone if she stood in the middle of the road. We made our calls as the only cars that we had seen all morning decided to whiz up and down that very piece of tarmac. We didn't linger; we were eager to get to the coast now.

We had noticed that we were hearing more and more Welsh spoken as we travelled west. We had anticipated this. Prior to our trek I'd bought a phrase book so that we could at least make some effort to greet and thank people in their own language. I had not been able to find a book easily so had ordered one, my selection being based entirely on size and weight. This is not the best way to choose a book. It claimed to have been produced in 1979, but if it had been thirty years older I wouldn't have been surprised. There was a whole section devoted to 'How to Meet Women'. This included sentences guaranteed to sweep a girl off her feet, such as, 'That's an excellent pair of breasts,' and 'Do you come here often?' Another page was for use when attending an eisteddfod and included the lines, 'Is that the Archdruid I see?' and 'Why is he wearing pyjamas?' Invaluable. I had learnt Welsh at school but after years of neglect it had not so much rusted as corroded altogether. All I could remember was 'We are going to the castle,' and 'Where is the small dog?' I suppose if pushed I could have asked the location of a small castle. So, we diligently practised our 'pleases' and 'thank yous' and 'call a vet'. I decided now was the time to use one or two of the choice utterances so as to better win over the natives.

Our opportunity came towards us in the shape of a tractor. The driver sweetly pulled over and switched off his engine. We cleared our throats.

'Diolch!' we cried.

'Diolch yn fawr iawn!' we went on.

He answered us with a blank stare and a small wave.

We tried again with the next driver.

'Aye, right you are,' he called back.

Aye? Were we in Scotland?

'We must be doing it wrong,' Nan said.

After that we thought it best not to speak until we were spoken to – in Welsh, that is. The brow of the next hill revealed a sight we had been longing for. 'The sea!' we cried in one voice. Now we really felt we were getting somewhere.

We trekked on to the village of Crymych, where we had been told there was a tack shop. We hadn't completely lost the ability to shop and hoped to find a whip for Nan, a wither pad for Holly, and a new girth for Sooty as his own was fraying rather alarmingly. People came out of their shops and houses to watch us as we clattered up the main street. We weren't used to this yet and felt more than a little conspicuous. We rode to the door of the tack shop and were hugely disappointed to find it shut. The four of us pressed our noses against the windows like children outside a sweetshop. All sorts of treasures were locked away inside.

A butcher emerged and ambled up the street towards us. He stroked Sooty's nose in the way only someone who has never touched a horse can. There are two places horses can't see, whatever position they are in. One is the back of the head; the other is directly under the nose. Sooty kept turning his head in an effort to see what was going on, the man kept touching his nose. In the end Sooty decided he must be being offered something to eat and opened his mouth. (He always worked on the principle of eat it first, you can always spit it out later.) Thinking he was about to lose his hand the butcher retreated a step. I suppose he usually met carnivores.

'Out for a ride, then?' he asked.

This is a difficult question to respond to politely.

'Yes,' I said, 'but we were hoping to do a bit of shopping first. Could you read that telephone number off the shop door, please? Perhaps we can see the lady who runs the shop later.'

He rattled off the number, which I scribbled on my map. I told him we'd come from Crickhowell and were currently heading for the coast.

'Don't they get tired?' he asked.

'We do let them rest occasionally,' Nan told him. 'Can you recommend a good pub near here?'

He pointed us in the right direction, probably convinced that the horses were fuelled by beer. The pub had a large, empty car park with wooden seats and tables. Perfect. We tied up the horses and I went inside to order some food. It took my eyes a while to adjust to the gloom. There were three people eating in silence and an elderly woman sitting behind the bar reading a paper. A clock ticked loudly. I ordered the drinks, which she fetched without saying a word.

'Could we have a couple of ham sandwiches, please?'

'Yes,' she said.

'And a bowl of chips?'

'Yes.'

'Can we have them outside?'

'Yes.'

I had to get more conversation out of her than this. I adjusted my riding hat pointedly. 'We've got two horses with us, you see. We didn't think we'd bring them into the lounge bar.'

'No!' she shrieked, falling into an ear-splitting cackle of laughter which made everyone in the pub jump. Well, all four of us. I fled with the drinks. We enjoyed a sunny lunch and a younger woman also provided buckets of water for the horses.

We continued west. The sun was hot again now. Sooty and Nan led the way as Holly and I dawdled along behind. My mind began to wander as the heat made me drowsy. I had never fallen asleep on a horse before, but I can now confirm it is possible, given the right conditions and an equally dozy horse. I only woke up when we came to a junction and Nan asked me which way we should go.

We arrived at the Croswell Horse Agency and Riding Centre at about five o'clock. Carolyn Morgan, the proprietor, was expecting us and greeted us like old friends, asking how our journey had been, enquiring after the horses' health and finding willing hands to help us untack. She agreed that Sooty's foot needed attention and gave us the number of a farrier.

'He's very good, but I don't use him because I can never get him to come when I need him. My blacksmith will be here on Monday, but if you want something done sooner than that, try this number.'

We put the horses in a shady, flat paddock inhabited by two black Shetland ponies. Surprisingly, the animals ignored each other completely. Sooty and Holly simply rolled and then got on with the business of eating. Nan found her phone worked beautifully if she stood on top of the muckheap. I left her there and wandered round the stables chatting to Carolyn. The yard was neat and tidy, every stable housing a well-loved horse or pony. The tack room was a shining example of order, with every saddle rack bearing the horse's name and bridles and grooming equipment arranged just so. It was a busy time of year for Carolyn, with as many lessons crammed into each day as was possible. She also took rides up onto the Preseli hills, which she told me provided some beautiful routes with views of the sea. I wished we had the time to explore further.

Carolyn offered to drive us into the little seaside town of Newport. We filled the boot of her fabulous old MG with our packs. I bagged the passenger seat and Nan perched on the back. She managed quite well until we reached the main road and got out of third gear.

'Can't breathe!' she gasped as she slid down into the front seat on top of me. Don't try this at home. Luckily it was a short journey. We arrived at the Golden Lion where we were booked in. I had anticipated us needing some creature comforts for our rest days, and was pleased to find the place so welcoming and the facilities just what we needed. The room was light and spacious with a decent TV, tea-making equipment and an en suite bathroom with a glorious, deep bath and a plentiful supply of hot water. We shared a drink or two with Carolyn in the bar. She introduced us to so many people we had no hope of remembering any names. The bar had a lively atmosphere with helpful, friendly staff. Later, after wonderful baths and a change of clothes, we feasted on one of the regular weekend barbecues. I'd never eaten so much meat in one week, let alone one meal.

We met some people who had been on a five-day, cross-Wales riding holiday. All of their luggage had been taxied on ahead of them, so they hadn't had to bother with saddlebags. They had had a great time, and envied us our three-week trip. One woman expressed her amazement at how clean and tidy we looked, and asked how we managed to carry with us everything we needed.

'Careful planning and packing,' Nan told her, waving a chicken leg for emphasis. I smiled to myself, remembering our weight and bulk selection system.

Feeling like party poopers we made our excuses and retreated to our room. We had been riding every day for a week and although our fitness level was improving, we were ready for a rest. We both felt a sense of achievement at having reached Pembrokeshire and the sea. Despite having the remote control in my hand, I fell asleep with the TV on and awoke far too late for breakfast.

Days Eight and Nine – The lion and the dragon

We rang Carolyn the next morning to check on the horses. She said they were fine and enjoying their time off. We had tried the blacksmith's number several times. We had spoken to his daughter and his wife and been told to ring again. We'd fared no better with the woman from the tack shop. Carolyn told us not to worry, asked us for a list of what we wanted and said she would give the details to one of her pupils who was going to a show where the tack shop woman would be. The items we required would be at the riding stables by Sunday afternoon!

The weather had finally faced up to the fact that it was August and the temperature soared. Newport is a delightful little town with interesting craft shops, galleries, cafés and restaurants. We bought postcards and presents for Nan's children, ate a delicious crab sandwich, and then headed for the beach.

Pembrokeshire has Britain's only coastal National Park. There is a coastal path from Carmarthen Bay to Cardigan Bay – a distance of some 170 miles. It's a marvellous place to walk. Parts of the coast consist of vertiginous cliffs; other areas open out into wide sandy beaches to rival any on the continent. There's plenty to please birdwatchers and wildlife enthusiasts. From certain points you could be lucky enough to see dolphins, and a short boat ride will take you to tiny islands inhabited by puffins and seals.

The quickest way to the beach in Newport is via the estuary. The tide was out as Nan and I walked towards the sea. We reached a point where the estuary had to be crossed. This meant wading through a stretch of water about two feet deep and ten feet wide. Simple enough, if you weren't carrying an unstable picnic bag over your shoulder, holding a camera in one hand, and a rapidly melting ice cream in the other. We made it across without the humiliation of falling flat on our faces, but it was a close thing.

The beach was glorious. Pale golden sand, sea a Mediterranean-blue, and enough space to be able to relax without some stray child building a sandcastle round your feet. It felt blissfully lazy not to be doing anything. We lolled happily for hours. Nan was toasting easily and I could expose my pasty flesh in safety since purchasing a large bottle of factor 24 at the local chemists. We toyed with the crossword puzzle, ate ready-salted kettle chips (with extra salt) and drank spritzers made of a wine that was most definitely not Liebfraumilch. Neither of us had brought a bikini. Well, it had been raining the day we packed. We improvised. It's amazing what you can do with a couple of scarves and some granny knots. Just don't make any sudden movements. Newport does not yet have a nudist beach.

Our peace was only briefly interrupted. A woman hurried by carrying a toddler who was screaming wildly. 'Poor little chap,' Nan muttered, instantly reminded of her own children back home.

'He's been stung on the neck by a wasp,' his mother explained.

'Waspeze!' Nan demanded, holding out her hand. It had become such a habit to take the first-aid kit with me that I still had it. We applied a couple of squirts to the relevant spot and the screams abated to silent sobs. He found the strength to nibble a crisp or two. His mother explained that he was always in the wars.

'We were in casualty with him the day before we came on holiday,' she said. I mentally ran through my medical supplies – bandages, sterile wipes, butterfly stitches. 'He's had open-heart surgery twice,' she added. I was defeated, despite my particularly sharp penknife. Just goes to show, no matter how well prepared you think you are, there's always the unexpected.

The little boy felt recovered enough to relieve us of a few more crisps and then they went on their way. I returned the Waspeze to my pack and took out one of my morning's purchases. It was a tiny red dragon, which I planned to pin to my saddlebag. The origin of the dragon as the emblem of Wales has its roots in Celtic mythology. The English may smugly imagine him to be the loathsome creature successfully defeated by St George, but he is an altogether different beast.

The story goes that King Vortigen was trying to build a fortress to keep out 5th-century Anglo-Saxons. He had stones collected for the purpose but each night they mysteriously disappeared, as if they had been eaten up by the ground on which they stood. Perplexed, the king summoned his wizard, Merlin, who explained that two dragons lived between the earth in this very place. Orders were given for the dragons to be dug up, and they emerged into the world of daylight, one white and one red. They fought, and the red dragon won. Merlin prophesied from this that the Celts would defeat the Saxons. The Welsh took the red dragon as their national symbol, and ever since it has signified their strength and determination to be free people one day.

Merlin's presence can still be strongly felt in Wales. His Welsh name is Myrddin, and the Welsh word for Carmarthen is Caerfyrddin. The town once sported Merlin's Oak, and it was said that if the tree ever died so would the town. A piece of hallowed oak is all that remains, preciously preserved in the Civic Hall. Merlin, like his pupil Arthur, has been credited with so many birthplaces and tombs; so many different provenances and fates; it is impossible to describe his life with any clarity. Only when we try to make sense of it do we remember that he is a figure on the cusp between myth and legend, and as such does not need the qualifications of date and place. The Arthurian stories contradict each other and even themselves, but what is undeniable is the importance Merlin held in the hearts of the ancient Celts and the enduring romance of this elusive magician. Even now it is spawning more books, films and followers.

Later we made more futile attempts to reach the blacksmith. When people at the pub heard who we were looking for they shook their heads and tutted, saying he was a hard man to find. I was beginning to think he, too, was a myth. By the next day we gave up and asked Carolyn if her farrier could do the horses the following morning. She said it wouldn't be a problem, and that things we requested from the tack shop were waiting for us at her stables. Amazing!

The Pembrokeshire coast

The second time we tried to get to the beach the tide was in. A pretty little stream had become a lake. We lazed on the grass, watching a shag dry its wings in the sun. It stood for over an hour on a piece of wood at the water's edge, its wings spread in a curious balletic pose. We listened to the omnibus edition of The Archers, though we had some difficulty picking up the right channel. Radio Dublin came through strongest. The best reception was with Nan positioning the radio on her tummy and keeping her left hand on the top of the aerial, elbow raised. Her posture was not unlike that of the shag.

My mother and stepfather took us out for a lovely Sunday lunch at Newport harbour. Despite the glorious weather and the charm of the place, the harbour and beach weren't overcrowded. It's a lovely place to potter about and relax, with its old stone walls, clean water, grass-covered cliff tops and abundant wildlife. My mother had brought fresh supplies of citronella, but we forgot to take it out of the car so it went home with her again. We visited the horses together, and everyone tried to say encouraging and reassuring things about Sooty's foot and Holly's sore bits. We would have to keep our fingers crossed that the blacksmith could reinforce both hoof and shoe somehow, or Timber would have to be sent for and we would reluctantly have to send Sooty home.

A cottage in Newport harbour

Day Ten – Boats and badgers

By the next day I was fidgety and ready to be moving again. Whilst the horses were being shod Nan and I went to the tourist information centre. Jane was extremely helpful, saving me dozens of phone calls by contacting her friends hither and thither until accommodation had been arranged for us and the horses that night.

We left the comfortable friendliness of the Golden Lion and returned to Carolyn's stables. Both horses sported new shoes all round – Sooty with an interesting 'toe-bar', which we hoped would protect his hoof and last the rest of the trip.

Carolyn was very busy teaching and the place was teeming with eager children tending their ponies. Sooty and Holly sighed heavily as we loaded them up with the heavy saddlebags yet again. We were happy to be able to reassure them that we had only a short ride that day and a special treat. We had decided to ride to the nearby village of Nevern, drop off our packs and then take the horses to the beach. We weren't sure if either of them had seen the sea before, but we knew they both loved water. We had already forded rivers and streams together, and Sooty in particular enjoyed a good splash and a wallow.

It was still hot and sunny and it felt good to be back on the horses again. They soon returned to their natural rhythm and we made good progress, quickly reaching the pretty little village of Nevern. I checked my map. We were looking for a cottage called Pontcarreg and I asked an elderly man for directions. He took time and trouble, making sure we were clear on where to go. As we rode on, however, his two, hitherto motionless, sheepdogs charged at the horses, snarling and barking. Holly leapt two feet in the air, landing almost on top of Sooty. The old man called to the dogs and they eventually slunk away.

'They don't like horses,' he remembered to mention.

We found Pontcarreg at the end of a narrow path. It was a fairytale cottage. Nan held the horses while I took the packs over the stone footbridge that crossed a silver stream into a beautiful, sun-kissed garden. The little white house nestled amongst the mallow, fruit trees, hollyhocks and roses. The lady of the house, Shirley Muntz, appeared and took me to a delightful ground-floor room that had French windows opening on to the magical garden. I looked forward to returning to such a lovely place later on.

We trotted along twisting lanes that rose up over a steep hill. When we reached the top we could see the shimmering sea below. Sooty stopped and stared. Holly stopped and ate some of the hedge, enjoying a juicy piece of cow-parsley. Sooty's head stayed unnaturally high as we began our descent.

'I think he's noticed it,' said Nan.

Indeed he had. The lane led to a car park that opened out onto the broad, flat sands. Despite it being six o'clock in the evening, there were still rather too many people on the beach for my liking. Sooty lowered his head for the first time in miles to snort at the strange, damp surface beneath his feet. People dragged dinghies past us and threw beach balls, and children ran about shrieking and squealing and generally making as much noise as possible. Sooty broke out in a cold sweat. Above him psychedelic kites flapped and fluttered; all around him small, high-pitched humans darted and danced; under his feet the ground moved, and ahead of him a great shining expanse of water hissed and splashed at him. He whirled around two or three times, reversing into Holly, trying to push her back off the sand. Holly herself was a little het up by it all, but seemed excited rather than frightened. We crept forwards towards the frothy surf. Sooty had grown, his paces relying on only the slightest contact with the ground, mostly on his toes. We somehow managed to hand an understandably wary stranger a camera. He photographed us from a safe distance, but even so Sooty's change in stature is obvious.

We tiptoed on. Sooty was trembling now. 'You know, he really doesn't like this,' said Nan, sounding much calmer than she felt. She was sitting on a time bomb and we both knew it. Had the beach been empty it might have been worth persevering. Possibly his love of water might have distracted him from the terrors which surrounded him, but the tide was out. The open stretch of sand in front suddenly seemed enormous – and far too populated. If Sooty panicked and bolted the casualties would be heavy. I doubted my ability to hold Holly if Sooty took off, and the thought of such a stampede through all those children and dozing sunbathers was too terrible to contemplate.

'I think we should very slowly and casually turn around and head back for dry land,' I said to Nan.

'I'm all for that,' she replied. We had both abandoned any ideas of horses frolicking in the salt water and cantering along the soft sand.

Beside the seaside

All we wanted to do was get off the beach without taking any victims. Nan tucked Sooty behind Holly, whose only thoughts were of food and rest now that we had turned for home. Those few yards back to the car park were some of the longest we'd ridden. So much for a special treat! Sooty didn't stop sweating and trembling until we had put several miles between us and the beach and the terrifying sounds of all that went with it no longer reached his twitching ears. He was nervous of boats for days afterwards, even if they were parked in a driveway.

We passed through Nevern again and found the farm where the horses were to stay. Some friends of Carolyn's had kindly agreed to let us use one of their paddocks. A blue-black Labrador called Pilot escorted us to the field. After a particularly vigorous bout of rolling the horses settled down to graze. At least Sooty's terrifying experience didn't seem to have adversely affected his appetite.

We walked back to the village; disappointed that what we had expected to be a lovely outing had turned into a nerve-wracking ordeal. Our accommodation helped to revive our spirits. Mrs Muntz had put great thought and care into the pretty little room. There were biscuits to go with the tea, coffee or chocolate; plump, springy beds; a decent-sized colour TV with remote control; a pristine shower room with the fluffiest of towels; a hairdryer and shoe cleaning and mending kits. There was even a box bearing the inscription 'Dammit, I forgot', which contained all manner of invaluable things.

We threw open the French windows and sat in the garden. Noticing some bowls put out on the grass and having admired some terrific photos in the bedroom, I surmised that we were in badger territory. We decided to keep vigil when it grew dark. We tidied ourselves up and headed for the local pub. Part of the Trewern Arms is a rather smart hotel with a frighteningly expensive menu. We opted for the more basic bar. It was alive with children and holidaymakers. The food was mass-produced and pricey. The salad had obviously been sitting around and had dried up and wilted. The chips were OK, but over £7 for a frozen chicken Kiev and a chewy radish or two seemed a bit steep. Still, the sea air had given us a thirst so we made good use of the bar. We would have enjoyed it more if we hadn't had to pick our way through the bits of food which adorned the floor. Between riding boot and flagstone, lettuce is slippery.

As we walked back in the twilight the village was a delight. A river spanned by a broad, curving, stone bridge runs through its middle, and a fragile mist rose from the meadows alongside the water and wrapped itself around the cottages. The church is quite impressive and boasts the oldest, and possibly most famous Celtic cross in Wales. It seems curious that a pagan symbol should have become part of a Christian church, but there it is. Nevern is on a pilgrims' route, and weary travellers would pause here on their way to St David's, holiest of cathedrals in the principality. How curious that their route should include a symbol of pre-Christian religion and belief.

We later learned that this seemingly prim and pretty village, which rests on its laurels of history, tradition and charm, also has a club offering nudist weekends for people of all sexual persuasions and preferences. If only we'd known at the time.

Back at the cottage we put out muesli bars and carrots in the badger bowls, crouched behind the French windows, and waited. Before we'd had time to get uncomfortable, a beautiful young badger trotted boldly up to see what sort of food was on offer. He didn't flinch at the automatic floodlight, but rootled about happily. If he was surprised at the strange meal that he found, he didn't show it. He seemed particularly keen on the tropical trail mix. I don't suppose he gets to eat dried mango and pineapple very often. He really was a fine specimen. I've lived in the countryside most of my life, but I'd never been able to observe a badger at such close quarters. Anyone wishing to see these lovely animals should definitely book a night or two at Pontcarreg. I'm sure they won't be disappointed.

Later, I studied the leaflets and brochures Mrs Muntz had provided for her guests. One of them gave quite a lot of information about Nevern church. 'We must have a look at the bleeding yew,' I said to Nan.

'What? I didn't know Mrs Muntz had any sheep.'

'No, the yew in the churchyard.'

'Well, what's it doing in the churchyard and why's it bleeding? Anything to do with those ferocious dogs we met?' she asked.

I wasn't making myself clear. I tried again.

'No, yew as in yew tree, not "ewe".'

She looked at me sideways, wondering if I'd overindulged at the pub. 'But you said that it was bleeding,' she pointed out.

'It is.' I waved a leaflet at her. 'Bright red goo has been pouring out of it since time immemorial. We should have a look at it tomorrow. Bound to be some sort of story attached to it.'

'Fine, fine,' said Nan, flopping into her bed, all but disappearing amongst the pillows, 'whatever you say.'

Day Eleven – Room at the inn

The next morning we ate the most delicious breakfast of the trek so far. We were getting used to making breakfast an important meal. Ever since the day of Nan's headache, and having encountered firmly shut pubs once too often, we knew the value of fuelling up at the start of the day. We ate fruit salad of melon and strawberries, a large bowl of cereal and an enormous plate of grilled bacon, sausages, tomatoes, mushrooms and fried eggs, followed by granary toast and home-made jam. Strong filter coffee washed everything down well. We sat in the early morning sunshine, enjoying the garden and chatting to Mrs Muntz. A nuthatch joined us, along with tetchy little blue-tits and a busy, staccato wren.

The wren often features in Celtic legends. Most birds had their place in the beliefs of the Celts, each symbolising something specific. For such a small bird, the wren had a deal of significance. To the Druids, indeed, it was the king of birds. The festival of midwinter would be marked by a wren hunt. This was the only time of year when killing wrens was allowed. Its death symbolised the passing of the old year and the birth of the new. Specifically in Wales, a wren would be put into a cage on St Stephen's Day, 26th December, and be carried around the village. The little bird was also seen as a potent symbol of fertility.

I asked Mrs Muntz about the bleeding yew. She told me one legend says that it will bleed until there is a Welsh king on the throne of Britain. I pointed out that Henry Tudor was born at Cardigan Castle and carried the Welsh colours at his coronation. Unfazed, she offered a second story, saying the tree started bleeding because of a vicar who was unjustly hanged. I later heard a third explanation – that the yew bled because the severed hand of a thief had once been nailed to it. Take your pick. Nan and I crossed the churchyard and had no trouble finding the tree, which does indeed ooze a remarkably blood-like substance. None of the other yews around it does so.

We walked back to the farm where the horses were staying, moaning about a slight incline and reminding ourselves how lucky we were to be riding and not walking through Wales. As always, Holly and Sooty came happily to us. We tacked up and rode back to Nevern for our packs. It was already hot and we had to apply liberal amounts of citronella to fight off the flies. The wither pad seemed to be staving off Holly's saddle sores, but the packs had worn a horizontal bald patch across her back. Luckily there was no sensitivity around the area. I readjusted things as best I could.

Outside the church is a splendid stone mounting block. Apparently the house over the lane had once been a coaching inn. We both struggled to manoeuvre our mounts close enough to the block to use it, lacking the necessary stable boy or ostler. We were able to fling ourselves aboard, but it was an inelegant business.

The road led us in a north-westerly direction across the low, rolling hills which fell away, billowing and soft, in all directions. The hedgerows now boasted exquisite yellow snapdragons, as well as an unusually pale heather, and cornflowers of blue, mauve and white.

Nan had opted for shorts, the weather being so good. She had a sheepskin cover on her saddle, but bare calves against stirrup leathers are an invitation to pinches so our progress was punctuated by sharp squeals. Sooty flicked his ears a few times, but then decided it was just another example of eccentric human behaviour.

We had a good sixteen miles to cover so pushed on, trotting on the

Stone mounting block

flat wherever possible. It was too hot to ask the horses to work hard uphill. We were leaving the Pembrokeshire Coast National Park now, and although the views were still wonderful, other subtle changes were noticeable. There were fewer shops, fewer brown heritage signs and fewer cars. Instead we met farmers working like ants in the fields to rescue their late hay at the end of such a bad summer. The first pub we found was closed, and the second tiny and not equipped for customers in any quantity. We were stepping out of a popular tourist area and into the emptier, lonelier stretches of the heartland of Wales.

We found a place for lunch with a yard just wide enough to reverse the horses into while we sat on the gate and ate rolls and crisps. Children from the local playing fields came to stroke Sooty's nose, something he had got used to by now. Both horses had lost a little weight but were looking sleek and shiny. They were managing very well on a constantly changing diet, though Holly's digestive system was still working a touch violently. They weren't accustomed to having hard feed, so unless we noticed any signs of exhaustion, lethargy, or a general dropping off of health. we thought it best to keep them on grass.

The heat was making us all drowsy, and the roadwork seemed hard. By the time we reached the outskirts of Newcastle Emlyn we were more than a little weary. Carolyn had given us the number of a friend named Janet with whom the horses would be staying for the night. We followed the directions we'd been given and were relieved when we finally turned up the track to Foel Farm.

'Janet?' Nan called out hopefully to the first person she saw. The figure emerged from under a large straw hat to reveal himself as a smiley young man. Obviously not Janet, he grinned and pointed towards the house.

Two more young men appeared, one being towed by a St Bernard. We asked for Janet. They shook their heads and told us their names and what a lovely day they'd been having and how lovely the horses were. A fourth young man joined us, laughing openly. It took a short while for us to realise that these friendly people were all in some way slightly handicapped. I'm not sure of the politically correct term to use, and have no wish to give offence. They were gentle and happy and welcoming, but Nan and I began to feel desperate as there seemed to be no one in charge, and more and more beaming boys joined the throng. At last Janet herself came out of the house. She was a large, smiley person, full of warmth, and happy to help two total strangers. Foel Farm is a residential home for people with certain learning difficulties, and she and her husband care for the residents. We led the horses past ducks and geese into a lush green field. I worried about the effect so much grass would have on Holly's stomach, but the horses needed a good feed, and anyway there was nowhere else to put them. They shared their field with two goats, which they ignored, being far more interested in eating. Janet's horses raced up and down the other side of the fence, showing off in front of the new animals. Holly stared at them in amazement, baffled by their unnecessary use of energy.

One of Janet's helpers drove us into Newcastle Emlyn to look for a room for the night. Everywhere we tried was full. In desperation I went into a particularly grim-looking pub. Unsurprisingly he had a vacant room, which could be ours for the bargain price of £25 including breakfast. 'We'll take it,' I said.

I dragged Nan and our luggage out of the car and tried to warn her that this just might not be quite as lovely as the place we had stayed at the night before. My misgivings deepened when the landlord demanded payment in cash before we had even seen the room. We struggled up the narrow stairs from the public bar. It was even worse than we had imagined. The furniture and decor were à la Pimlico bedsit, circa 1956, and the room may not have been cleaned since that date. Everything was covered in a layer of grime. Nauseating objets d'art on the tiled fireplace were not improved by the cigarette ends stuffed into them. The bedclothes were prison issue grey stripes. The wallpaper had several layers of bilious greeny-yellow paint flaking from it. The low ceiling added to the depressing feel of the room, as did the hot, stale air and small, all but opaque window, which we had to wedge open with a withered geranium from the window box.

'Well, it's cheap,' I offered.

'It's OK,' said Nan. 'It'll do, it's a place to stay.'

'It's only for one night, after all.'

'Yes, it's fine, really,' Nan persisted.

We stared at the ghastliness of it all. 'No, it's not fine!' I squawked. 'It's disgusting! It's horrible!' I sat heavily on the bed, which sank beneath me to the accompaniment of twanging springs.

'At least we don't have to worry about our sweaty saddlebags making the place dirty,' Nan was determined to look on the small, dim-but-bright side.

'Let's get a drink and find somewhere to eat,' I said, beyond any thoughts of baths or hair washing. We trailed up and down the high street, peering into equally gloomy pubs and wondering why on earth

Dear Timber,
We have just visited Pembrokeshire. We went to the seaside — it was horrid! This big puddle kept hissing at me, and lots of squealing little children ran at me with boats and kites and balls. It made me sweat and tremble a lot.
Wish you were here...
...and I wasn't.
Hopefully see you soon,
love from Sooty x

PEMBROKESHIRE EYE

© Pembrokeshire Eye Photo. Tel: (01646) 66464

Timber
Llangenny Riding Centre
CRICKHOWELL
Powys.

7037

Lovespoons carved by W. E. Williams
Printed by Haven Colourprint, Pembroke Dock

Celtic Camera

My Dear Angela,
These people I'm with don't seem to know much about anything — including where we're going, where we've been, or where we are. I'm doing my best to hold things together. Luckily the food is adequate — please send bia-calm.
I've met a perfectly charming donkey. I never did know his name, we just had the one special night together.
Hoping this finds you as it leaves me.
Kind regards, Holly.

Michael Cutter Photography 06839 42377

Mrs Angela Ralph
Llangenny Riding Centre
CRICKHOWELL
Powys.

PRINTED IN WALES

C.C. 18

we'd come to this godforsaken place. To our astonishment we found a little Italian restaurant. It was an oasis of brightness, with its fresh red, white and green tablecloths, white walls and cheerful staff. We eagerly ordered some very palatable wine and a garlicky chicken concoction which made a welcome change from the usual pub fare. The wine worked on our exhaustion and near-hysteria to reduce us to helpless giggles. The waitress even asked us to stop laughing so much at one point. Over coffee we composed postcards. Holly wrote one to Angela, her owner, while Sooty's was for Timber, our reserve horse back at Llangenny Riding Centre.

Day Twelve – Llanybydder

We were keen to leave Newcastle Emlyn (or Gremlin, as we had re-Christened it). However, our hopes of an early escape were thwarted by the tourist information centre not opening until ten o'clock. We used the time to stock up on essential chocolate supplies and hunt down some new bags which could be attached to our saddles, as, however hard we tried not to, we accumulated more and more things-we-couldn't-do-without. I'm still not sure what they were. I lost Nan at one point. This takes some doing in a town with one street, but I managed it. As I enquired after her in one shop, the man behind the counter shook his head.

'Are you sure?' I persisted. 'She was wearing spurs.'

He raised his eyebrows. 'I haven't seen anyone wearing spurs today,' he replied, as if he had yesterday and might tomorrow.

I dived into the tourist information centre as the lights were being switched on. The well-dressed lady in charge produced a book showing all the local bed and breakfast places. When I say 'all' I mean those accredited and recommended by the Welsh Tourist Board. The centre offers no information on any other establishments. This can be extremely frustrating. There are hundreds of lovely places to stay which do not meet the exacting standards of the Tourist Board, but you try finding them! Also, each information centre only covers a local area, which we were invariably just about to ride out of. However, I had to find us somewhere to head for, so I wasn't about to give up. Our route would pass through Llanybydder – famous for its horse sales – so I tracked down the phone number of the auctioneer's office. As I wasn't calling anyone from their book I couldn't use the centre's phone, so I stomped off to a phone box feeling we might as well not have waited for the TIC to open after all. Mr Evans of Evans Bros, Auctioneers, was, in contrast, extremely helpful. He was happy for the horses to spend the night in his own meadow in the centre of the small town, and recommended a pub where Nan and I might get a room for the night. Accommodation details finally sorted out, we ordered a taxi and made our way back to the horses.

Sooty and Holly looked considerably fatter than they had done the night before. They ate the proffered carrots out of politeness. Sooty was standing up to the erratic feeding regime well, but Holly's stomach was still giving cause for concern. I decided that if we were faced with such lush grass again we would have to tether her to try and limit her consumption.

The hot, sunny weather raised our spirits as we finally left Newcastle Emlyn. We had a hilly route of about fourteen miles to cover, with some nasty bits of main road. We were cheered up, however, by the sight of the Cambrian Mountains in the distance, approximately two-days' ride ahead.

Sooty's new shoes and toe-bar afforded him the protection he needed, and the new bags fitted easily onto our packs so we were able to trot on steadily. The horses were very stoic about the traffic. One motor bike whipped past us doing about a hundred miles an hour, his slipstream ruffling the horses' manes. One sideways step at the wrong moment would have resulted in carnage, and almost certainly one dead biker.

By a stream we found a little pub declaring hot and cold food served all day. We were delighted to discover rings to hitch the horses to in the car park. Perfect! Not so perfect was the promised food. It was two minutes to two, and a lot of places closed the kitchens at two. I rushed inside.

'Have you stopped serving food?' I asked breathlessly.

'We never started,' said the landlady.

'What?! But the sign outside...'

'I used to do lunches,' she explained, 'but circumstances change, don't they?'

If I never eat another cheese and onion crisp again it will be too soon.

We trekked on. There were some days when the going seemed difficult and the journey long, and this was one of them. We missed the rolling hills of Carmarthenshire and the beauty of the Pembroke coast. The traffic was fast and dangerous, watering holes few and feeble, and Holly was lethargic and unwilling. I had to constantly urge her on to keep up with Sooty. Even putting her in front didn't raise her interest level. I think her stomach must have been pretty uncomfortable, and she was picking up on my bad mood. I tried to focus my thoughts on Llanybydder. The horse sales there are well known, particularly for their Welsh cobs, which are paraded up and down at high speed. The last time I had visited a horse sale had been at Abergavenny Market. There is a constancy and timelessness at these markets. The first thing you notice is the vehicles – vans, trailers, cattle lorries, horseboxes - all trying to disgorge their cargo of anxious animals. It is obvious to anyone that there is not enough room for them all, but in they come. The harassed man in charge of parking waves people backwards and forwards throughout the day as they inch their way into spaces which just aren't there. Somehow it all works. Somehow horses are unloaded and put into pens or tied to a piece of string, which is tied to a piece of rope, which is tied to anything heavier than a horse, from a Land Rover to the window of the market office.

The horses themselves are an eclectic mix. There are, of course, handsome cobs, broad-fronted and sturdy, available in a variety of rich, deep colours. Holly's distant cousins are to be found in every third pen. A few proud, graceful Arabs flare their nostrils at passers-by. Groups of mountain pony yearlings, recently separated from their mothers, huddle together wide-eyed and afraid. People throng between the pens and among the vehicles. It is a miracle nobody is trodden on or squashed as mothers wheel pushchairs all but under some of the horses. An impressive cob stallion has been brought to…well, advertise his services. His burly, red-faced owner puts him through his paces. Together they charge up and down a wholly inadequate piece of tarmac, strides getting longer and longer, legs a blur, handbrake turns inches from the abattoir wall, appreciative nods and smiles from the crowd.

In the auction ring an old brown mare is being led round at a shuffle. The auctioneer starts slowly enough, reading from the catalogue.

'…quiet to box, clip and shoe. No vices. Good in traffic. Has seen hounds. A fine mare, ladies and gentlemen, a safe conveyance. What am I bid, then? Who'll start me off? Do I hear five hundred?'

There is a respectable pause before the first invisible bid is made. The auctioneer, his eyes tuned to the secretive twitches and tics that indicate money offered, picks up the signal and then he's off. Bidders or no, his speech is machine-gun fire to rival any agitated Italian.

'Five-hundred-I'm-bid, five-hundred-five hundred-five-fifty, five-fifty-I-have, do-I-hear-six? Six-hundred-on-my-left, six-fifty-six-fifty-six-fifty, seven, seven-fifty, eight, eight-fifty-eight-fifty-eight-fifty-I-have.'

He draws breath. The mare whinnies in the pause.

'Eight-fifty, the-bid-is-on-my-right, com-along-now-l'dies-'n'-gen'lmen, who'll-give-me-nine? Nine-hundred, nine-hundred-nine-hundred-nine-hundred.'

Another pause. He raises his hammer.

'Are you all done?' Bang, the hammer falls. 'Sold! For nine hundred guineas.' He turns to his assistant. 'Rhys, Llanwern Farm.'

Outside, negotiations move at an altogether different pace. Two farmers stand beside a dozing chestnut cob. The owner holds the rope of her startlingly white halter, purchased minutes before from the stall a few yards away. He leans back against the bars of the pen behind him. It's important not to look too eager to sell. The prospective purchaser rests an elbow on the horse's rump as he sucks at his empty pipe. It's important not to look too eager to buy. To start with they talk about anything other than the horse. They discuss the absence of rain as if it were of note in high summer. They comment on old Mrs Pritchard having finally passed on in her eighty-fifth year. They exchange views on the wisdom or otherwise of the new twenty-four-hour garage on the edge of town. All this is done with such a sparsity of words you'd think quotas had been imposed on them. After a pause for reflection the buyer finally raises the subject of the animal.

'You've 'ad a foal from 'er then?'

The owner looks at the mare as if for the first time. 'Aye, smart little colt. Foaled easy she did.'

Another pause. 'Good doer, is she?'

This means, will she stay fat and sleek on poor grass and mouldy hay.

'Well, aye. I give 'er a bit of cake in the winter, but she doesn't need much, you know.'

'She looks quiet enough.'

'Oooh aye, the kids used to ride 'er, an' all. Good in traffic too, mind.'

As if to emphasise her amenable nature he lets go of the rope, flicking it over her neck so that she is standing loose. The mare is asleep now, bottom lip drooping, and has no intention of moving an inch. A lengthy silence follows. These wordless moments are crucial to the whole process. A rule of thumb, should you ever find yourself in this game of nerves, is to rely on the eloquence of silence. When you feel like speaking, wait. When you've waited as long as you can, stay silent a little longer. Hopefully the other person will crack before you do and commit himself to some comment or question you can then deal with. It is not for the faint-hearted. I've witnessed an inexperienced buyer filling the gaps with ceaseless chatter, a sweat breaking on his brow, his enthusiasm and discomfort raising the horse's price and lowering its age with every third word.

The negotiations have now reached the knowledge stage. This is where the buyer inspects the horse to show that he knows what he's about, and the vendor resumes leaning on the pens to show that he knows nothing amiss will be found. The buyer, pipe still clenched between teeth, runs his hands down one of the mare's legs – the nearest one will do, never mind if one the other side is made of wood. He picks up her hoof and taps it with his pipe. Satisfied with this rigorous test he checks her teeth, without waking her up. Next he walks slowly round her, lifting her tail and peering briefly underneath. What does he expect to find there? Washing instructions? Finally he steps back a few paces as if looking at a large painting which needs some distance to be fully appreciated. A skewbald pony ridden bareback at breakneck speed flashes past him, brushing his shoulder. His gaze does not waver from the chestnut mare. He resumes his original position.

'So 'ow much d'you want for 'er, then?'

Another silence you could drive a coach and four through.

'Well, I dunno.' The owner pushes back his flat cap and scratches his head. This sets up a reflex similar to a yawn and the buyer does the same. They replace caps and stand in contemplation.

At this stage the observer could go and get a cup of tea, visit the tack stalls and circle the market. He would miss nothing, but return to find them talking about something completely other than the horse. Eventually, after several lunges and parries, one of them will mention a figure. The other will revel in this show of weakness. If it is suggested by the vendor, the buyer (after, naturally, a suitable pause) will declare that he hadn't thought to pay so much for her. If the figure is put forward by the purchaser, the owner will suddenly become sentimental about the animal and insist he couldn't part with her for so little. The crucial point comes when the opposition puts in a counter figure. Now they both know that a fair price lies somewhere between the two amounts mentioned. In some cases the buyer will mutter something about the high price and then wander off. This by no means indicates that he has decided not to buy the horse, he may well return later to pick up where he left off. Buy in haste and your money will be spent on someone else's leisure.

On this occasion, however, the owner plays his trump card – he offers to throw in the tack. The unwary should hold their excitement in check at this point. The saddle, if such it can be called, will certainly be at least twice the age of the horse. It will have seen leather oil or saddle soap three times in the same week once a year on the whim of a succession of fickle children who soon after discovered Sonic the Hedgehog and never sat on a horse again. It will have been stretched and squeezed to fit everything from a Shetland to a Shire and consequently be as flat as a pannier, its tree now several unconnected pieces of wood. The stirrups will be odd and the leathers different lengths. In short, it is an instrument of torture for both horse and rider. The bridle will have lived a parallel life.

Of course, our canny buyer knows all this, but the quality of the psychological advantage he now has over the seller is much more valuable. Now he makes his final offer, the owner reluctantly agrees and the horse is sold. The buyer then digs into his coat pocket and counts out the correct amount of money from a thick wad of notes. If he is an expert these will not include fivers, so that when the ex-owner has to hand him back some luck money it will be at least a tenner. Twenties would be too much and he would be in danger of ending up with a handful of coins.

The rope is tied to a piece of string, which is tied to... The two men, their business concluded, at last able to talk in their more natural garrulous manner, head off to the pub together to celebrate having done the auctioneer out of his commission.

Llanybydder itself is a small town nestling in the Teifi valley. The broad river sweeps silently through it. We found The Black Lion, which is situated next to the market, where we were able to tie up the horses while we untacked and unpacked. Inside, the pub resembled the Marie Celeste. I wandered about, carrying my saddle, and calling out to anyone who cared to hear. The doors were all open, the television on in the bar, but no one appeared in response to my cries. I was in the kitchen before I found anyone.

'We've a room booked for tonight,' I explained, feeling even more out of place than usual in my hat and boots, loaded with tack, standing next to the fridge. A lively, red-haired girl showed me where we could put our tack and handed me a key before disappearing again. Still, it wasn't a very big place so presumably we'd be able to find the room unaided.

We led the horses over the wide stone bridge and down the public footpath to the meadow. The bank to the river was steep in parts and boggy in others. We could only hope the fire brigade would not be necessary to rescue the horses from it the following day. Once again we had to trust to their common sense.

Back at the pub we located our room. The rather attractive stripped oak door was not, sadly, an indication of what lay behind it. Three large beds were crammed into an area that would better have housed two. There was, as had been promised, a television but it was of the black and white (or rather grey and snow) variety and on a table so low you would have to sit on the floor to watch it. At least this meant the picture quality mattered less. As if to balance things out the window was so high up that even standing on the bed you couldn't see out of it. A small shaft of light fought its way in. The en-suite shower room did have a window you could reach, which was propped open by an empty beer can. Oh, joy!

We headed out to see what Llanybydder had to offer in the way of something to eat. The first place we came to looked promising but they had just stopped serving food – it being ten past eight. At this point we had to remind ourselves that it was we who were out of sync with everyone else. We were the odd ones out. Clearly none of the locals had need of food so late. We were the ones that had to learn to fit in, and not expect the world to fall into place around us. The next pub didn't do food, but two men let go of the bar and took the trouble to come outside to point us in the direction of one that did. We gratefully wolfed down lasagne and chips, to the accompaniment of German football commentary (via satellite TV) and Welsh chatter. We were the only women in the pub, and very obviously the only non-Welsh speakers. Nevertheless, we were made to feel welcome, and the men were happy to forgo the football to pore over our maps and suggest a good route for the following day.

By the time we reached our comfortable beds back at the Black Lion the window and the cardboard towels seemed unimportant. The friendliness of the little town and its laid-back attitude to life had won us over. We had, after all, in part come here to escape the hectic pace of our own existences. How much better, then, to relax into the local rhythm rather than fight against it.

Day Thirteen – Lured away by beautiful strangers

The next morning people emerged from somewhere in the building to present us with an enormous breakfast. Someone in the pub the night before had given me a name and number and after a couple of brief calls farmhouse accommodation was arranged for the four of us. We had a short ride ahead so were able to take the time to seek out Mr Evans to thank him for the use of his meadow. Despite it not being a market day, the office was full of people and activity. An elderly gentleman told us how the horse sales were still well attended with many different breeds available. He asked us about our horses and seemed satisfied when he heard at least one of them was a Welsh cob. Mr Evans kindly refused to take any payment for the horses' grazing and wished us a good journey.

The horses had managed to resist falling into the river or getting stuck in the mud. Both looked content and well rested. As usual, they came eagerly up to us, accepted their carrots, and allowed themselves to be led off for another day's work. A lot of horses I have known would at least have put up some pretence of not wanting to be caught.

We had taken the bridles to the field with a view to riding bareback to the pub to tack up. This seemed appropriate. There was a wonderful photo in the auctioneer's office of a young lad doing a butcher's-boy trot through the streets on a fiery cob with nothing but a bit of string to control it. Getting on was not a graceful sight, and we were thankful we weren't being watched as we wriggled and squirmed our way aboard. The horses were surprisingly bony, and it was difficult to stay in place. We hoped Sooty wouldn't choose this moment to shy dramatically at a drain. Fast trotting was definitely out so we made our way gingerly back to the Black Lion. We found the market being washed with a pressure hose, to which both horses took exception, so we tied them to a bench-table combination outside the pub.

A family of small children and their mother piled out of a nearby car and came rushing over to squeal at the horses in Welsh. By now Sooty and Holly were well used to this sort of attention and had grown to quite like it. A woman in an apron came out of the baker's and made a fuss of Holly. She explained that she and her husband often went on long-distance rides on Exmoor, and helpfully gave us the phone number of someone who might help us further down the road.

We had decided on two short days as a possible rest day was a long way off. This allowed us the chance to amble along at an easy pace and not to have to ask much of our mounts. We made a brief stop for a drink before pressing on towards Lampeter. Now we could clearly see the Cambrian Mountains beckoning us. We meandered along sun-dappled lanes, stopping to take photographs and let the horses pick at the hedgerows. We still hoped to see a red kite, but could only find buzzards.

We rode through the centre of Lampeter, a medium-sized town on the Teifi, and boasting its own university. The horses drew a lot of attention as we walked down the high street. When we stopped at a pelican crossing the pedestrians forgot where they were going and surrounded us with pushchairs and trolleys to admire Sooty and Holly. The horses didn't mind, but the drivers we were holding up became understandably impatient. Nan spotted a particularly interesting shop so I parked the horses in the supermarket car park while she nipped in for a quick browse. We took up only one bay and there were plenty of spaces, but we still had to move when a woman with the weekly shop on her mind insisted on parking where we stood. Seeing our packs another shopper exclaimed that she had never thought of coming to Sainsbury's on a horse, but what a good idea it was.

Nan soon returned clutching her purchases (which were, naturally, small and lightweight) and we were on our way again. This is not one of the most spectacular parts of the country nor the prettiest, but the narrow valley on the edge of the Cambrian Mountains has its own charm. For me its appeal is its honesty, its reality. This is not Wales tidied up for the tourists. It is as kempt as it needs to be for farming land and, yes, the inhabitants take a pride in their gardens. But there is no cosy façade. Barns are built for their functional efficiency, with little thought given to the aesthetic. Fences and hedges keep stock in or out, but are not photo opportunities of hedging expertise or drystone walling. Being on lowland pasture, we were back in dairy country again, which meant fields full of cows (Friesians mostly) and somewhat muddy lanes.

The weather was cloudy and muggy as we turned up the drive to Nant-y-Medd. This was definitely a working farm. The house itself was freshly painted and set against a pretty garden to one side and

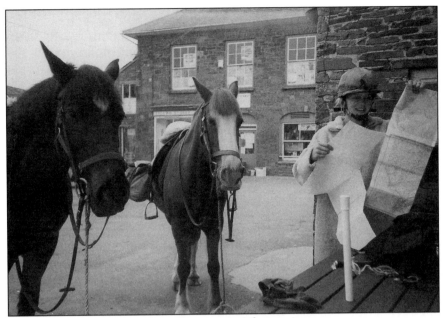

One of us can read the map!

shady oaks around. Behind it ran the trickling brook which gave the place its name – 'stream of honey'. The yard was wide and partly grassed over. It was formed by a rectangle of barns and sheds, some stone and old, some breeze block and new. Two tethered sheep dogs gave the alarm as we approached and Elinor Evans appeared, flanked by a small terrier and a laughing spaniel.

Dogs feature frequently in Celtic myths and legends. Mostly they are hunting dogs, though they were also used in war, to protect people and property, to kill rats, and as companions. They appear in stories of both mortals and inhabitants of the Otherworld. The first part of the *Mabinogion* (the ancient collection of Celtic tales written in Welsh) features a hunt where two packs of hounds belonging to different masters chase the same stag, with far-reaching consequences. The Celts saw dogs as portentous symbols, which could foretell health, war, or the presence of an immortal.

Elinor's dogs were of the earthbound variety. The spaniel, it turned out, had come from across the valley, decided it enjoyed Elinor's company, and stayed. The collies were working sheepdogs and never ventured into the house. I passed an opinion on the Yorkshire terrier.

'I think he's too big to be a vegetarian,' Nan said.

At least, I'm sure that's what she said, but she continues to claim she said 'Yorkshire terrier'. I thought it strange at the time that she should know so much about the dietary habits of a dog she'd only just met.

Elinor was a small, curvy woman in wellington boots, and layers of clothing held neatly together by an apron. She had thick, wavy, brown hair and sparkly eyes. She took to the horses at once and was very much at ease with them, chatting away to them in Welsh while we unpacked. We followed her to the shady paddock at the back of the house. There was sufficient grass and a little stream supplying drinking water and a chance for the horses to muddy their feet.

The farmhouse was long and low with bedrooms built into the roof. We were given an extremely spacious and comfortable room with an adjoining bathroom. Nan and I both took advantage of the time in hand and the facilities to take long baths and change into our skirts and sandals. It was such a refreshing treat to get out of our riding clothes. Elinor prepared a delicious, three-course evening meal for us. It was excellent value at £9 each, all beautifully presented, expertly cooked and in generous helpings. Stuffed, Nan and I repaired to our own little sitting room with our coffee and studied the guidebooks and leaflets provided. One bed and breakfast place I read about described itself as always offering a warm welcome, and made a point of mentioning it had a fire certificate. When I asked Elinor if she would recommend it she told me it used to be very nice but had recently burnt down!

Like many of the ladies we stayed with, Elinor was a widow. As a farmer's wife and a mother her life had been full and busy. Now she was on her own, though her son still ran the farm and her daughter grazed her horses there. Having guests was clearly not simply a source of extra income for Elinor but an interest, giving her the opportunity to share her home with appreciative people, many of whom came back every year.

Nan and I were happily lounging in front of the television when Elinor arrived, wide-eyed, at the door. 'Where are your horses, then?' she asked, as if they might be in the sitting room with us. 'The gate's open, and they're not in the field.'

'You're joking,' I said.

She was not. We dashed outside. The yard gates were open, and the horses could have easily reached the main road, but surely one of us would have heard them clattering past the house. We grabbed headcollars and checked the field. The knot I had tied in the thick rope securing the gate was still done up, but the rope itself had broken.

'Perhaps the trotters came down,' Elinor suggested.

It turned out that her daughter's prize-winning trotters roamed the hundred-acre farm and often made their way down to the farmhouse in the evening. Following hoofprints, we trudged across the fields. To our dismay several acres were covered with eye-high thistles, and there we were in our skirts and sandals. We picked our way painfully uphill, alternately calling and cursing. After a steep climb the land flattened out into a grassy plateau. In the very farthest corner we could just make out some equine shapes in the fading light.

I could quite see why Holly and Sooty had been lured away. The two trotting horses were dark-eyed, beautiful bays, with graceful heads and elegant long limbs. The four stood quietly as we put headcollars on our rather sheepish-looking nags. We spent the descent trying not to get our vulnerable feet trodden on. Of course the trotters didn't want to be separated from their new-found friends and we ended up with everybody milling about in the yard. There followed a ridiculous ten minutes of opening and shutting gates and trying to herd the right animal into the right place. Elinor took it all in good part and did her best to help. Now we were faced with what to do with Sooty and Holly for the night. We couldn't risk putting them back in the same field. It was decided that Elinor would move her pet Welsh Mountain pony from the small patch next to the garden, and our horses could go in there.

The little grey pony was about three years old and had been rescued from the meat man at the market when a foal. Elinor put a rope around his neck and led him through the garden. Or rather, he led her. Thoroughly lit up by all the activity in the yard, the pony leapt and plunged as Elinor clung to the rope. She made him stand still for a moment and remonstrated with him in Welsh. They proceeded across the yard steadily for a few paces before he erupted into a series of rodeo bucks. Elinor hung on gamely, letting out peals of laughter which only served to spur him on. They shot into the paddock, her wellington boots a blur over the ground. I slammed the gate behind them, she slipped the rope from his neck and he sped away, doing cartwheels round the field. Elinor returned, still laughing. Sooty and Holly watched impassively as if the whole thing had nothing to do with them whatsoever.

We pushed them into the tiny area behind the garden. There was not a blade of grass, just a few docks and weeds. They looked at us in horror as we double-tied the gate behind them.

'It's your own fault,' I told them, 'this is what you get for eloping with beautiful strangers.'

Holly eyed the lawn longingly. Sooty leant all his weight against the worryingly low fence as he strained to reach the runner beans. I had visions of waking up to find the garden demolished. We left them sulking among the docks. We apologised to Elinor for the trouble they had caused.

'Oh, don't worry,' she cried, 'it's all a bit of fun, isn't it!'

Nan and I went upstairs to tend to our thistle and stinging nettle wounds. That night I dreamt of giant Yorkshire terriers eating their way through fields of runner beans.

Day Fourteen – Gold!

The next morning was grey and drizzly. We closed all watertight doors and put the horses in the yard, where there was actually quite a lot of grass for them to pick at. Sooty made straight for the flimsy bit of fencing between him and the slurry pit. I watched him lean on it as he reached for some particularly lush grazing on the other side. Elinor telling me how they had recently had a cow fall in the pit didn't comfort me much. Nan was convinced Sooty had more sense so we went and had breakfast. It was every bit as tasty as the meal of the night before and we put away huge quantities. Our appetites had certainly improved during the ride. I normally start the day with a cup of tea and a cigarette, and could never have imagined myself eating a full English breakfast every day. I thought guiltily of the horses' empty tummies.

We were thankful we had only a few hours' ride as the weather had worsened significantly. We borrowed a towel (belonging, I suspect, to the Yorkshire terrier) and made feeble attempts to dry the horses' backs before tacking up.

The lady I had been told to contact had, sadly, died the year before. After a slightly embarrassing conversation on the telephone with her son, the four of us were booked in at the Talbot Hotel, Tregaron. It had stables behind it, and hay and straw would be provided for the horses.

It was raining steadily as we waved goodbye to Elinor. When she called after us to come back again with the horses, any time, we knew she really meant it. Sooty shied at every drain, tried to snatch food from the hedgerows, and generally fidgeted the whole way. Clearly he was hungry and blamed us. Holly just lowered her head, turned her ears against the rain, and plodded on. After a few miles we were all thoroughly wet and fed up. The countryside around us may have been pleasant, but it was too murky to see. We were stuck on the worst type of B road. It was barely wide enough for the cars, but everyone drove along it as if it were a dual carriageway. Stopping at a village shop proved hazardous as the building opposite was being sandblasted. Not only was it impossible to make oneself heard, but the horses decided they'd had enough and refused to stand still, walk forward or co-operate in any other way. It was clearly a day for just covering the miles and getting to where we had to go. Not having the luxury of waterproof maps, my little piece of precious paper soon disintegrated into papier mâché. Luckily Tregaron was signposted, so at least we didn't have the irritation of getting lost added to our day.

Tregaron is a strange little town. It has half a dozen or so shops arranged around the square, a couple of banks, a post office and a tourist information centre (yippee!). The main focus of the square, however, was the imposing, grey-stone Talbot Hotel. It was easy to imagine large meets outside on Boxing Day, a scene which would have been little changed for a hundred years or more. At the back of the hotel was a neat row of small, low stables, two of which had been cleaned out in our honour. How nice and snug, we thought. Sooty

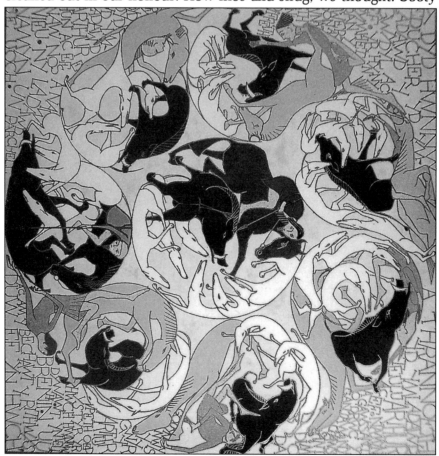

One of 12 champlevé designs by Peter Lord

was not so sure. To be fair, they were on the narrow side, and once enticed in he had difficulty turning round. Angela's account of him hurling himself over the door to escape such confinement came back to me.

'It's no good,' I said, 'we can't leave him in there. He'll either get cast or try and escape.' We examined the area around the stables. A small strip of concrete led to a grassy patch of about a quarter of an acre with a spacious loose barn. We cleared it with the proprietor and then turned the horses out. They were delighted with the grass and tucked in straight away. We put some hay in the barn for them to nibble when they got fed up with the rain.

Log fires crackled and blazed in the cosy, flagstoned bar of the Talbot. We treated ourselves to a lunchtime gin and tonic and sat in the window, toasting our toes in front of the fire and watching the rain bouncing off the pavements outside. It was the right day to be indoors.

Tregaron's growth was based on sheep. All around it, on the lonely moors and high in the exposed hills, stone farm cottages peppered the landscape. The wool from the area had been well known, as had the sheep themselves. Years ago the drovers would take them east to England to get the best prices possible. Indeed, a shepherds' bank was formed early in the nineteenth century – Banc y Ddafad Ddu – The Bank of the Black Sheep. Perhaps the choice of name was a mistake as the bank collapsed owing money to many farmers who may never have recovered from their losses.

Tregaron has a small museum giving information on local history and a kite centre. The only kites we'd seen so far were made of plastic, attached to long pieces of string, and anchored to the ground by a small child. We decided to hold out for the real thing. The red kite is used as a symbol throughout the region and we felt we must spot one soon or we'd be the only people in Ceredigion who hadn't.

An attraction we did make for, however, was the Welsh Gold Centre. This is a splendid shop specialising in the gold and silver jewellery of Rhiannon. The gold is Welsh and comes from the nearby Gwynfynydd mine. It's available in different carats and very pretty, if a little pricey. The silver versions are just as lovely. The designs are based on Celtic art and mythology and are really beautiful. The shop also houses an excellent selection of good quality crafts and gifts, as well as an interesting range of Welsh books (some in Welsh). It's a wonderful place to browse and I defy anyone to leave the shop without buying something. We came out with armfuls of cards, some silver love spoons, books and presents for Nan's children.

All this necessitated a visit to the post office. I'd wrapped my parcel, but wanted a large, strong envelope to put it in. The man behind the counter peered over his spectacles and shook his head.

'Ooh, no, we haven't got an envelope that size,' he said.

We stood and looked at each other. I needed to post a parcel and I was in the post office. It was no good leaving – if I couldn't succeed here what chance had I got anywhere else? 'Well, what can you suggest?' I asked. 'I really do need to post this today.'

He scratched his head. Time passed. At length an idea came to him. 'I have got a large padded envelope.'

The parcel was posted. I still can't decide if he was trying to be difficult or if he was simply vague. After all, I hadn't indicated that any sort of envelope would do, as long as it was the right size.

My next task was to get some route details faxed to me. A working fax machine proved to be almost as elusive as a red kite. The post office didn't have one, the TIC was shut and the one at the hotel was broken. The Gold Centre came to my rescue. I noticed with interest that all the staff there chatted away to each other in Welsh, even the teenagers. It was encouraging to hear the language being used so naturally and easily by a younger generation.

I succumbed to a second browse and bought a card showing the accompanying illustration. The scene depicts a hunt, a recurring theme in many Celtic stories. The intricacy of the design and its flowing, continuous pattern is a fine example of the unbroken ribbon or thread which is found in Celtic art. Horses, hounds, stags and boars are creatures one might expect to find in Welsh folk tales, but how about mice? One of my favourite stories is that of Manawyddan and Pryden, from the *Mabinogion*.

Manawyddan had been given seven estates of Dyfed by Pryden, and was growing a fine crop of wheat. When the time came to harvest it he went out in the morning to find the stalks had been stripped bare from one field, with not an ear of wheat left. He was at a loss to understand what had happened. The next morning he found the second field in the same sorry state. He decided to hide and watch and find out who was laying waste to his crop. In the middle of the night a plague of mice appeared, running through the wheat, devouring it as they went. Manawyddan slashed at the mice with his sword in fury, but they merely swarmed around him, too fast and too many for him to fight. He noticed one that was slower and fatter than the rest and caught it. In his anger he decided to hang the mouse as a thief. As he was preparing to do so a number of passing strangers tried to stop him, promising him money, but he would not be dissuaded. Finally, the magician Llwyd arrived, begging for the mouse's life. It was he who had changed his army into mice and sent them to ruin Manawyddan's crops. On the third night his wife had expressed a wish to be sent with the others, to experience being a mouse and play a part in the destruction of Manawyddan's land. But she was heavily pregnant, which is why she had been fat and slow. Eventually, Manawyddan agreed to release her as long as all the spells were lifted from his land and everything was returned to its original state. The wizard agreed and got his wife back, and Manawyddan was able to live in peace as his land became fertile and abundant again.

Later we went to see how the horses were. In fact, it was our habit to check the horses every evening if they were staying within walking distance of us. On this occasion, after the events of the previous night, we were more anxious than usual to check that all the gates were securely shut. The horses had filled themselves with sweet grass and were standing in the loose barn snoozing. They had eaten only a little of their hay, so we returned to the welcome warmth of the hotel bar to eat our suppers with a clear conscience.

Day Fifteen – Magic mountains

The dining room was packed for breakfast, mostly with foreigners – which I suppose is what we might have been considered ourselves. Nan requested ham and scrambled eggs for a change and was given such an enormous plateful we squirreled some of it into our packs for lunch. We took advantage of the nearby shops to buy some rolls and tomatoes and a bottle of wine to complete our picnic. We were to continue north on a ride of approximately twenty miles over the mountains, so it seemed wise to take plenty of fuel with us.

The horses allowed themselves to be tied up. The sun had come out and the day promised to be quite hot. We noticed Holly and Sooty were both shaking their heads a lot and close inspection revealed a revolting infestation of something like forest fly, though we were a fair step from the nearest copse. These disgusting creatures burrowed down inside the horses' ears where they bit them until they bled. We reached for the citronella. Holly stood patiently whilst I practically poured it into her ears and the flies came buzzing out. Sooty was less keen, but after a short struggle Nan doused the necessary parts. We then (and please, don't try this at home) took the hoof pick and carefully hooked out any lingering flies. Holly let me brush the insides of her ears gently, too, but Sooty drew the line at this. After a frantic ten minutes the head shaking stopped. Holly let out a long, appreciative sigh of relief.

We were surprised to find so much traffic on what looked on the map to be a small road. Every second vehicle was towing some sort of trailer or other, so we surmised there must be a show up ahead. It was disappointing to find that the drivers who rattled past us the fastest and closest were those transporting horses. If they couldn't be trusted to be more thoughtful, who could?

The road soon became narrower and steeper. We were climbing up from the valley through a series of small villages, along a route that would eventually take us up over the hills to Devil's Bridge.

We had noticed a marked change in the horses' level of fitness. Angela had put extra roadwork into them before the start of the ride, and they were used to working for their living, but we had been asking something extra of them. Ten to twenty miles a day, with only one

A between-the-ears view on the way to Devil's Bridge

short break, over two weeks, had tired them at first, but now they had increased stamina, and, provided they ate well enough, were finding the going easier. As were we. Spending several hours in the saddle every day, being in the fresh air most of the time, frequently lifting heavy packs, and eating well had all contributed positively to our energy levels and physical fitness. The beneficial effects on our mental well-being were undeniable, too. Although we may have had the odd stressful day, and what we were doing was both physically and mentally challenging, Nan and I never once argued or lost our tempers with each other. A difficult moment was soon forgotten when we turned the corner to find another breathtaking view, or smelled wild honeysuckle, or encountered a friendly, helpful stranger. The willingness and stoicism of the horses made us thankful to be with them every day. The sheer act of getting up each morning, setting off in a new direction to an unknown place and travelling across such a magical landscape gladdened the heart. Added to which the escape from our everyday lives was blissfully refreshing. For me, no rush-hour tubes, city noise and fumes or long hours at work. For Nan, no getting children off to school, fighting with life as a single- parent family, worrying about having enough change for dinner money or a sponsored this and that. For a few weeks we were free.

We came to the village of Pontrhydigiad, which was comprised of a few small houses, a wide bridge and a pub. Sooty automatically turned left into the pub car park, which was all the persuasion Nan and I needed for a pit stop. We had been practising interval training to cover the miles from Tregaron. Walk for three minutes, trot for three minutes, walk again. The horses accepted this rhythm quite readily when asked now.

As the horses dozed in the shade and we sipped our drinks in the sun, a hum and a rush of white noise preceded a loudspeaker announcement from the other side of the hedge. A tuneful Welsh version was followed by a heavily accented English one, 'Good morning, ladies and gentlemen, and welcome to the Pontrhydigiad Annual Show. It's wonderful to see such a good turn out, and the weather has been kind to us so far. We hope you will all enjoy your day. The first class will be under way in the main ring in ten minutes, so could competitors please make themselves ready. That's Class One, for section C Welsh cobs, restricted to local competitors.'

Nan and I looked at Holly and wished we'd brought some hoof oil with us. The commentator went on, 'Remember, please, this class is only for those coming from less than three miles from Pontrhydigiad.'

Damn, we thought, we've just hacked 4½ miles. Oh well, it would have been embarrassing if Holly had walked off with a prize anyway. They didn't have any classes for Dales so Sooty was denied the chance to shine, too. We might have done well in a Trekking Class.

The road from the village climbed steeply, and beautiful open vistas revealed themselves. Just as we reached the top of a particularly sharp incline I let out a shriek.

'A kite! A kite!' I pointed feverishly.

'Where?' Nan demanded, expecting yet another buzzard.

'Over there, behind those trees.'

We both dropped our reins, shielding our eyes against the sun, craning our necks, swivelling in our saddles.

'Are you sure?' Nan asked.

'Yes. You know how everyone said we'd know one when we saw it, well I know! Look – there!'

And there it was, at last, and it was fabulous. Not at all like a buzzard, really. It looked as old as the landscape and as wild and free as the Welsh mountain wind. We sat and gazed at it while the horses mowed the hedgerow. The beautiful bird wheeled and swooped for a few, fleeting moments before taking to the clouds and disappearing. We rode in silence for a while after that, enjoying the memory of the kite, uplifted by it. It was only when the scenery around us seeped into our minds that we were moved to speak again.

The countryside here was different again from any we had ridden through before. The mountains were huge and high, with wiry grass and patches of rock and heather, but they were rounded at the tops, fat and curvaceous. Thin fences enclosed them all, so that what appeared as wilderness was, in fact, farmed and owned. This was clean land, grazed, and at times even ploughed, to the very tops. And dotted over it, in irregular clusters, as far as the eye could see, were gleaming white dots that could have been stones or mushrooms, but were sheep. The whole effect was of a naive painting. And the distances, the glory of the space opening up all around us, were food for the soul. Up here the earth was tamed and tended, but still it felt free. In every direction the blue horizon was so far away it faded and blended with the sky. Between those unfathomable points and us lay the warmest, most magical landscape I have ever encountered. It was not the sweet patchwork of lowland Carmarthenshire, nor the rugged, hostile, dramatic peaks of the Brecon Beacons, but a third beauty, another sort of splendour. More than ever, I wished I could paint. Why do we so desperately want to capture and hold and possess something wild? What is it in us that urges us to make a two-dimensional image of something which has as its essence the third and fourth dimensions? With relief, as the country unfolded before us, I realised that I had no need of holding this wonder in the palm of my hand, reduced and flattened, a shadow of its reality. In my mind I can go there any time I want now that I have experienced the place, absorbed it, felt its ancient, timeless heartbeat. It is not mine and never will be, but I belong to it, wherever I am.

I noticed, too, that the whiteness of the sheep was actually to do with their being a different breed from those we had seen before. Back in Crickhowell there were little Welsh ewes on the hill farms, with the occasional merger with Suffolk or Leicester, whilst the ugly, coffee-table-shaped Texels had recently been imported into the lowlands. While heading west we had seen more Texels, with Welsh sheep only on the hillier bits, and fewer Suffolk crosses. Here we were surrounded with speckle-faced sheep similar to, but smaller than, the Kerry. They had appealing black noses and snowy white wool. They were quite bold and often stared at us as hard as we stared at them.

The day wore on and our shadows grew longer. Thin, dark shapes, more flattering versions of ourselves and our horses, rode beside us on the uneven ground. The flowering grasses, fescues and reeds glowed pale gold now in the afternoon sun. We passed an old lead mine, long closed, sealed and grassed over. All that remained on the exposed plateau were a few ruined stone buildings and unnatural depressions.

Small farms and lonely cottages kept a respectable distance from one another, and many had forgone the chance of tarmac road for the slower approach necessitated by a rough, stone-strewn track. Trees were few, and those there were clung together in faithful pairs or small groups, bracing themselves against each other, holding their breaths for assault by the icy gales which gave them all a common list. The nearest village to the mine was several calf-aching miles away. Workers could be spared the climb if they opted for the dormitories constructed at the pit. Having seen pictures of their austere, chilly interiors, I think I would have taken the walk home.

Along the way we came across what looked like a Welsh pony stud. Leggy foals, tails high, scampered about their mothers at the sight of us. One, who appeared to have been weaned already, came hurtling up to the fence and whinnied at us in a shrill, desperate

Wild Wales

voice. His heavily lashed eyes wide and nostrils flaring, he followed us until stopped by a gate as the lane turned away from his field. His heartbreaking cries echoed around us for a long time after he was out of sight.

We zigzagged down a few hundred feet and joined the main road for a mile or so before turning off to Tyn Castell. The farm's name means house of the castle. We later discovered this had nothing to do with an actual building, but referred to the small, strangely shaped hill which overshadowed it. Its silhouette did indeed resemble turrets and castellations. We met a man in a Land Rover who directed us up to the house where his mother, Lizzie, was expecting us. She was another farmer's widow. One son worked the farm, and the other was an electrician.

Lizzie was a formidable woman who didn't give away smiles lightly. She showed us where we could put our tack, and the horses, tired now from a long, hot, hilly ride, stood quietly and patiently as we fiddled with buckles and baler-twine. Lizzie and her rangy teenage grandsons took us to the paddock. It contained an interesting collection of sharp, spiky farm implements, which many horses would have impaled themselves upon the minute our backs were turned. By now we knew Sooty and Holly had more sense. There was also a large duck pond (with ducks), surrounded by a reedy marsh, but there was a clean edge at which the horses could drink. There was plenty of tasty grass, which they set about mowing at once. Lizzie was disappointed.

'I thought they would kick up their heels and gallop off,' she said.

'They've had a hard day,' Nan explained. 'The only thing on their minds now is food.' This about summed up how I felt too, but there remained the questions of where we were going to eat and how we could get there.

Back at the house we were joined by more of Lizzie's family. Over a cup of tea we explained that we would need similar accommodation the following day. We discussed the area we were heading for and everyone contributed ideas of who might help, or where there was a bed and breakfast place. The discussion was conducted at high speed and mostly in Welsh. Lizzie's son, Edryd, slipped into English now and again to try and keep us informed, but after a while he forgot. Amazingly, a childhood spent praying and singing in Welsh at every school assembly seemed at last to be paying off. It was as if some deeply buried treasure had shaken itself free of mud and floated to the surface of my memory. I couldn't utter a word, but found I could follow the conversation and interject in English. Phone calls followed and beds were found for us, while a field for the horses was left pending.

We asked Lizzie for the number of a local mini-cab firm to take us to the nearest pub. The whole family gasped in horror. We couldn't possibly go to that pub – it had recently (three years ago) changed hands and was now run by some very peculiar and unwelcoming people. They didn't say whether or not they were English. The next pub was a good seven miles away, so walking was out. We were told this was no problem. Lizzie said she hadn't been out to dinner for ages and would drive us to the right place. This was a kind offer, but I have to admit to a less than charitable sinking of two hearts. It was lovely to spend time with new people and get to know them, but we had had a long ride and felt neither interested nor interesting. Besides which, I found Lizzie quite terrifying and didn't think I'd be able to relax and eat with her watching me. I know this sounds horribly ungrateful and ungracious, but it's how I felt at the time. Perhaps so many hours spent with the horses in semi-wilderness had made me unsociable and less civilised. Most of the time we certainly looked as if we'd gone bush.

But, there it was, we could hardly refuse. We tidied ourselves up as best we could and clambered into Lizzie's car. We passed the first un-acceptable pub, which looked pretty good to me, and sped on. We crossed the high bridge that gives the place its name. Deep in the gorge below ran narrow, fast water, force-fed from the popular water-falls hidden in the woods. We travelled on across more open moor-land. Lizzie said yes, all the hills were enclosed and owned, and no, there weren't many bridle paths, and yes, most people were sheep farmers. I was pleased when we reached the Castle Inn. My relief turned to dismay, though, when we discovered how crowded it was. We sat in a room where American and English children all but bounced off the walls. Nan said if she had to listen to children she would rather it were her own, and went off to phone them. Lizzie drank orange juice. We had large gins. It was impossible to have a conversation with all the shrieking and shouting going on around us. After a few minutes I could stand it no longer. Lizzie had been sitting, impassive and inscrutable, until I tentatively suggested that maybe she'd prefer a quieter table in another room. 'They shouldn't let them behave like that,' she said. 'No child of mine would.' I believed her.

We finally came to rest under the air-conditioning unit. We put our jumpers back on and sat in silence, waiting for Nan and the food. Both arrived together. The food had a dramatic effect on Lizzie. She tucked in, remarking on the quality and quantity of her selection and enquiring after ours. The alcohol loosened our tongues and something one of us said tickled Lizzie. Her face was transformed by a radiant smile and her shoulders shook with silent laughter. After that there was no stopping her. She seemed to find delight and amusement in everything. I began to wonder if she really had been drinking orange juice. Possibly her initially stern manner was born of shyness, and now she had relaxed and was enjoying herself a different, warmer side was revealed.

The food was plain but well prepared and tasty. Gradually the children dissolved into the night and their noise was replaced by a gentler pub murmuring. Lizzie regaled us with details of the lead miners' lives. Her parents had told her about those times as she had been only a young girl when the place closed down. It sounded like gruelling work for long hours in poor conditions. Now most people scratched a living out of sheep or tourism. Edryd, she declared, worked very hard as an electrician. She also spoke with unchecked pride of her grown-up granddaughter, who had gone to work in New Zealand. Prior to that she had lived at the farm with Lizzie, and it was obvious how much she missed her. Later, a large delegation from Lizzie's family appeared in the pub. Edryd was amongst them and he told us he was still working on finding a field for the horses for the next night.

Back at the farm, we thanked Lizzie for taking us. When we told her we had enjoyed our evening we genuinely meant it. Just as we were climbing the stairs she floored us by asking if we needed two beds or if we would be OK sharing one. Neither of us could fathom the thinking behind this. Was she trying to save on laundry, or did she have the wrong idea about the relationship between Nan and me? We replied that we would, actually, prefer separate beds, if that was all right. Her expression was once again unreadable as she showed us to our room.

Day Sixteen – Ice cream Sunday

The next morning we were ushered into the hitherto unseen dining room. Generations of Lizzie's family gazed down from the walls as we tucked into a lovely breakfast. Edryd arrived to tell us that a field had been found and gave us a contact name and number. Soon we were off again, under a warm but cloudy sky. The horses were as well fed and rested as we were, and the few miles of main road we had to start our day with were mercifully traffic-free.

Great excitement was caused by Nan's mobile phone ringing. It was the first time we had been able to get a signal since Newport. There were thirteen messages waiting for us. Several were from somewhat irritated people asking why we bothered to have a phone if we never switched it on. None of them could have conceived of the idea that we had been in a signal blind spot for six days!

The skyline now had a new configuration. We were in windmill country. These were not quaint, Quixotic constructions, but space-age, modern configurations. They stood a measured distance from each other like so many anorexic versions of their older cousins, waving their shiny blade arms. I was reminded of War of the Worlds. They looked as if they might uproot themselves at any moment and come striding towards us.

We left the main road and minced our way down a ridiculously steep lane that would lead us to the river valley. To our right we could now see one of the waterfalls, a silent, silver ribbon falling from the very top of the mountain to the hidden river below.

I had read about a local narrow gauge railway which transported visitors from the coast to the waterfalls and back again. I had checked the times, and if we weren't careful we were going to reach the small level crossing to coincide exactly with the passing of the train! Sooty and Holly had proved themselves to be pretty brave (seaside aside), but we felt even they might baulk at a steam train. A whistle warned us of its imminent approach.

'How far are we from the railway line?' Nan asked.

I checked the map. 'Oh, I think it's behind that hill. We're quite safe here.'

'Are you sure?' The whistle blew again as Nan spoke. 'That sounds pretty close.' The horses had heard it too. They raised their heads, ears swivelling, and began to tiptoe.

'Don't worry,' I reassured Nan, 'if it was close we'd be able to see the steam.' This seemed a reasonable idea to me. We walked on, rounded a sharp bend, and found ourselves standing on the railway track.

'Ah!' I said.

We looked left and right. No steam. No train. At that moment the whistle blew again, clearly very close. Both horses forgot to snort at the tracks and shot over the level crossing.

'Shit!' said Nan. 'We must have missed it by seconds.'

We let the horses trot on briskly until they felt they were well away from whatever it was in the woods. I later found out that, due to forestry fire regulations, the train was in fact diesel, and so produced no steam. This is the sort of detail it would be helpful to know in advance.

We stayed with the river until we reached the village of Capel Bangor. As the pub had no car park we tied the horses to the church gates. Their girths loosened, they immediately rested a foot and dozed. The church was unusual, being more chapel-shaped, and spire-less, but it was clearly a church and had heavily leaded, stained-glass windows.

We sat eating our sandwiches and sorting out our phone messages. An elderly lady appeared. We were afraid she might complain about our choice of hitching rail, but she had come to admire the horses. She explained she had been a keen rider when younger, but hardly ever saw riding horses now. She remembered a young girl coming to stay on her parents' farm one year. Her mother was salting a pig but had run out of salt, so she sent the visitor into the village on a quiet pony. Unsure of what was required; the girl bought the largest bar of salt on offer and balanced it precariously in front of her on the saddle. All went well until it began to rain. What started as light drizzle developed into a heavy downpour. By the time the poor girl reached home she had only a piece of string and one extremely salty pony to show for her trouble.

The woman shrieked with laughter as she recounted this tale. She asked us lots of questions about the horses and what we were doing, and was so taken with Holly I thought for a minute she was going to ask for a ride. But instead she wished us well on our journey and thanked us for letting her see the horses.

Lots of people came up to touch, pat, or just talk to the horses. It surprised me that so many of them said they hardly ever saw a horse, given that we were in a predominantly rural area. Most of them chatted to us, but there were others who behaved as if we weren't there. They would chat away to Sooty or Holly, either touching them on the nose timidly or slapping them heartily on the neck. Then they would walk away.

We left the valley and twisted up through a maze of lanes barely wide enough to ride along side by side. Sloping pastures rose up either side of us. Occasionally we glimpsed more windmills, much closer now, tall as pylons and emitting a menacing whine. One group had been planted practically in the back garden of a little farmhouse, and loomed above it. I wouldn't want to sleep in their shadow. One is torn between supporting a clean, safe method of energy production, and crying out against the ugliness of its presence.

In sharp contrast to this unnatural view, we were treated to a brief sight of a pair of red kites. One precious glimpse, a flash of bronze feathers caught in a shaft of sunlight, and they were gone.

We came across a garage with a spacious forecourt and decided to indulge in an ice cream or two. The horses and I waited by the compressed air, all rather hoping no one would choose that moment to use it, and Nan trotted off to rootle through the freezer. The sun had fought its way through the clouds and felt warm on our backs.

It is strange how quickly one becomes blasé about manoeuvres on a horse that might previously have seemed daunting. We walked briskly into the village, ice creams in hand, Nan checking her mobile phone and me checking the map. We weren't holding the reins with any care, and were getting away with it up to the point where Sooty brushed against the hedge and rattled a wasps' nest.

'Wasps!' I cried unnecessarily, waving my Mivvi in the air. This succeeded in exciting the wasps further, so our only option was to outrun them. We tore through the village, clinging to map, phone and ice creams, holding our reins by the buckle, clattering, Bonanza-style down the street. It wasn't until we'd done a sharp right and a sudden left that we shook them off. Nan's Cornetto fared quite well, but poor Holly was wearing most of my Mivvi, raspberry goo and vanilla ice cream dripping from her mane. There was a stickiness about both of us for the rest of the afternoon.

We negotiated a busy section of main road and finally reached the Black Lion at Talybont. An attractive pub, it stands on the far side of a rare village green. Though common enough in England, there are few to be found in Wales. The pub was smothered in flowers, which burst out of tubs and hanging baskets in a carnival of colour. We left our packs and rode on the couple of miles to the horses' field. We were quite near the coast again now. At one point Sooty started displaying some quite alarming and uncharacteristic behaviour. He refused to go forward, kept whirling around and running backwards. It was a few moments before we worked out what the problem was. He could see the sea. He must have remembered that the last time we travelled without the packs and headed towards the gleaming, flat surface of the distant giant puddle, we had gone to the beach. He did not want to repeat one of the most terrifying experiences of his life. We put Holly in front and persuaded him to follow, but he jogged and shied at ghosts in the hedge.

We were pleased to find that it wasn't possible to see the sea from his field. This was a ten-acre, flat area; well grazed, but with sufficient grass. The field also contained an enormous, skewbald cob. It was clearly fed up with being on its own and charged up to the gate to greet us. We spent an anxious fifteen minutes watching the horses together. Holly tried to get on with the business of eating, but the skewbald wouldn't leave her alone. Sooty was having none of this, Holly was his mare, and no lumbering, wall-eyed stranger was going to touch her. He placed himself firmly on guard, flattening his ears and lunging, teeth bared, at the other horse if it came too close. The skewbald was persistent, and the exchanges became more and more aggressive. Luckily, the skewbald wasn't shod, and Sooty was pretty good at avoiding his flailing hooves. When they both stood on their hind legs and threatened to have a fully-fledged stallion fight, we began to panic. It had taken an endless chain of people to find this field, and it was a bit late in the day to start looking for another one. We held our breath as we watched. Sooty made one particularly vicious dive at his rival, sinking his teeth into its ample rump, and this seemed to settle the argument. The skewbald withdrew to a safe distance.

Ron, the proprietor of the Black Lion, kindly collected us and drove us back to the pub. He showed us to our comfortable room, and we made arrangements for him to take us back to the field in the morning.

Nan opted for a quiet night in and I went to have dinner with my godmother. Maddy is an agronomist, and has lived in nearby Aberystwyth for years. We hadn't seen each other for more than two decades and I couldn't help but be amazed by the different pace at which we had lived our lives over that time. She had lived in the same house, in the same, small, seaside town, working at the same place, married for seventeen years to her recently deceased husband. I had moved house more than twenty times, lived in different countries, had a dozen different jobs, and don't sit comfortably in the same sentence as the word 'husband'. Maybe coastal West Wales had had a stabilising influence on her.

Later, as Nan and I lay in our beds worrying about the horses, our thoughts were interrupted by raised voices downstairs. A man was vehemently cursing and swearing, while someone else tried to calm him down. Shouts and cries were interspersed with sobs and wails. Doors slammed, and the anguished man went outside, continuing to rant. Now he was standing directly beneath our window and we could make out the words. 'I'll kill her,' he screamed. 'Bob Evans (not the real name) is dead meat!' A tragedy unfolded in a sentence. Clearly not everyone in the area lived a tranquil life.

Day Seventeen – The enchanted wood and the dry CAT

The next morning was grey and drizzly. We ate a good breakfast and Ron ferried us back to the horses. We checked them over. No bites, no kicks, no fighting injuries. They did seem a little unsettled though. They both refused to stand still while we tacked up. We thought perhaps they were still nervous of the skewbald, but he was at least eight acres away. On closer inspection we discovered tiny, lice-like creatures in the horses' hair, particularly around their tummies. We used up the last of the citronella, but even that didn't seem to help much. 'Let's get them out of here,' said Nan.

We hadn't gone a hundred yards before something large, stripy and stingy attached itself to Sooty. I managed to swipe it with my map. By now both horses were extremely fidgety and not being their usual co-operative selves at all. Things just seemed to get worse. We

Oh! The glamour of it all!

had trouble finding the right turning off the main road and my packs refused to stay in place. Holly insisted on snatching mouthfuls from the verge, which I found particularly irritating. We eventually found the right lane and scuttled up it. My packs slipped again and I struggled to right them. Holly made another grab at a bit of cow-parsley, making me drop my whip. Something in me snapped.

'Right! I've had enough!' I screamed. I jumped off, let go of the reins and let fly a stream of abusive language at Holly. She stared back at me, mildly surprised. Clearly something in the tone of my voice told her not to push me further. She stood like a standing stone as I heaved the packs back into position and adjusted straps and string. I climbed back on board.

'Better now?' Nan asked.

'Much,' I said, then blushed crimson as I spotted someone gardening on the other side of the hedge. I don't normally scream at my horse, I wanted to tell her, really I don't. Holly behaved meekly for the rest of the day, and I even found myself apologising to her in a quiet moment later on.

On the map we had spied a tempting bridle path which would cut off a long stretch of main road. Experience had taught us not to attempt to go 'off-piste' unless we had local confirmation that the route was clear, but we had made up our minds to try it. We found a lovely grassy track and indulged in some gentle cantering. Even the packs had decided to co-operate and stayed in place. We passed a derelict cottage and entered a dense, fragrant wood. Just when the day was starting to improve, we saw something which was enough to make both of us scream. Ahead, completely blocking the beautiful, turfy path, was an enormous fallen tree. It was too low to get under, and much too big to attempt to jump! There were sturdy fences either side and not a gate for miles. My feeble little wire-cutters were useless. Nothing short of a chain saw was going to get us through.

We retraced our steps and studied the map again. Neither of us could face even more main road, so we wandered through the woods, following our noses, and praying we would rejoin a lane at some point. I was beginning to think we should have left a trail of pebbles in case we had to find our way back again when the trees parted to reveal a cottage and (hooray!) a small lane. We picked up our route and pressed on, knowing that we still had eighteen miles or so ahead of us. The horses began to settle into their work and we trotted and walked, trotted and walked, for several miles. The sun had come out, causing a deal of stripping off and re-packing of wax coats.

We passed through a small farmyard. An extremely old woman made her painful way towards us. She smiled at the horses. 'Oh, there's lovely!' she beamed. 'I wish I had some carrots for you,' she told Sooty. Then to us she said, 'I used to ride when I was a girl. Do you know, I've been thinking lately how useful it would be to have a horse. I can't drive, you see, but I could get about with a nice quiet cob. Trouble is, I don't know how I'd get on. That's the problem, you see.'

We could see. The thought of her trying to heave her stiff, frail frame into the saddle, and then to be bounced and jogged about, made me wince.

'What about a little trap or cart?' Nan suggested. 'That might be more comfortable.'

'Well, yes,' she said, 'you're right, I suppose.' She grinned. 'Not the same, though, is it?' She gazed lovingly at the horses. We asked her if the lane we were on would take us through the narrow Llyfny Valley, over the hill and back to the main road at Machynlleth.

'I suppose it will,' she said. 'Haven't been up there myself for years, mind, but yes, I believe you can get through that way.' We thanked her and waved goodbye. It was hard to believe she hadn't ventured up the very road that went past her house for years. We wondered if she ever went anywhere anymore.

'We'll be like that one day,' Nan said, gloomily. 'Unable to get on a horse, and nobody to take us anywhere.'

'Thanks for that cheery thought,' I said. I hadn't mentioned to her the problem I'd been having with my ankle for the last two days, but what she said made me see it as a momento mori. I think the trouble stemmed from Holly's wretched saddle. Despite the new wither pad, it was still flattening horribly and tipping me forward. This was shifting my weight and with all the trotting we'd been doing the result was a painful, stiff and swollen ankle. Why only one ankle was affected I couldn't say. More and more I found myself kicking my foot out of its stirrup at every opportunity. For the last two nights the swelling around the joint had made it difficult to get my boot off. I had even resorted to rising trot without stirrups, which did wonders for my thigh muscles but was bloody hard work. Holly's trot was too uncomfortable to sit to for more than a few strides, so my options were limited.

We followed the lane through a gate and into a wood. This was not a modern pine plantation, but an ancient, overgrown, enchanted place. The canopy of green above let through sunbeams that landed on glowing ferns and luminous mosses. The ground fell steeply away to our left, down, down, down through the trees to an invisible stream that we could only hear at this stage. The lane was tarmac, covered in a layer of lichen, moss and water, a lethally slippery combination. Sooty skidded constantly, and Holly's stride got shorter and shorter until I decided to get off and lead her for a while.

It was a beautiful place. The road slowly descended to meet the river, which raced and gurgled, foaming over gleaming pebbles and flat rocks. Curious grasses grew on the woodland floor, resembling nothing so much as hair, hanging in gold-green clumps. The jewel-like colours and furry textures of the mosses made us feel that we were riding over a living animal, something curled up, slumbering. We tied the horses to a second gate, which signified the end of this delightful wood. There we sat, watching the water swirl and surge, whilst we nibbled our sandwiches. The pain in my ankle was difficult to ignore now, and I was glad of the wine we had packed for our picnic.

A lazy hour later we set off again. Leaving the wood behind us, we wiggled our way round and over a small, steep hill. At the top we stopped to take in the landscape. Our high perch afforded us a wonderful view. To our left we could just make out the sea, distant and too faint to worry Sooty. In the valley below lay the small town of Machynlleth, and in front, rearing up to the sky, was the first of a chain of spectacular hills and peaks, cliffs and valleys, that made up the Snowdonia National Park.

Within half an hour we were in Machynlleth. I liked the town, and rather wished we had been able to plan a rest day there to investigate further. But time was running out. We had hired the horses for three weeks, and would soon have to return them to Angela. We had considered a circular route before the start of our trek, but decided there were more important things than starting and finishing in the same place. We wanted to cross the Beacons, the Black Mountains and the Preseli Hills. We were determined to go to the beautiful Pembrokeshire coast. The wild reaches of the Cambrian Hills were a must, and our ultimate destination had to be Snowdonia. To have ridden a loop would have meant sacrificing one of those, and we weren't prepared to do it. This meant we had only a couple of days' riding before we would have to take the horses home, so an overnight stop in Machynlleth was out.

The town was bustling as we rode down the main street. There were lots of people shopping or browsing or simply wandering about. There was a good selection of interesting shops housed in attractive, old stone buildings either side of the wide road. The horses took it all in their stride, and we found the car park easily. Nan stayed with the horses while I scuttled off to the tourist information centre. It was a very smart example, in a lovely, stone-walled, terraced building. There were crafts, cards and books galore. I gathered up leaflets and brochures advertising places to stay, and bought a map of the region. I had bought all the necessary maps weeks before the trip, but had inadvertently posted one home when jettisoning some ballast from my pack. On my way back to the car park I stopped off at the supermarket to buy a bottle of wine.

On my return I found Nan entertaining a throng of excited children. They all wanted to pat, stroke, sit on and kiss the horses, and she was trying to meet their requests without anyone getting squashed or trodden on. We could have topped up the coffers by charging for rides, but I don't think Sooty or Holly would have thanked us.

At last the children drifted back to wherever they had come from. I sat on the tarmac making phone calls. We had somewhere to stay for the night, but I was keen to find us something a bit special for the following couple of days, as that would mark the end of our journey. I leafed through the brochures, searching for a country hotel that just might have a field. I had put the wine in its carrier bag on the ground next to me. For no visible reason it suddenly keeled over and smashed, disgorging its contents in one expensive glug. Nan and I stared at each other in disbelief. Wordlessly she binned the remains and trudged off in the direction of the supermarket. I continued with my phone calls. It was only as I was booking us in somewhere that I noticed that the horses weren't actually tied to anything, and I wasn't holding them. They were just standing there, patiently waiting for us to stop messing around before moving on again. Little stars.

As we left Machynlleth (and if you're not Welsh, please don't try pronouncing this) we crossed the river Dyfi, and let out a cheer as we passed a sign telling us we were entering Snowdonia. A sharp right, right again, then left had us following the river north up a dark, narrow valley. The land on both sides was crowded with trees, small paddocks and cottages, so that it felt cramped and slightly claustrophobic. We had become accustomed to lofty views and wide-open spaces. Somehow this groove in the mountains was not pretty and magical like the Llyfny valley, but rather depressing.

We were anxious to find the horses some water as they had had a hard day and the sun was still quite strong. We were frequently near streams and rivers, but not able to get the horses close enough for them to drink.

We stopped at a cottage and hammered on the door, but no one appeared. Sooty rather pathetically sucked a dried-up puddle. Checking the map I could see that we would soon be at the Centre for Alternative Technology. I have always liked the idea of this place and felt sure it was the shape of things to come. It said on the leaflet I had acquired from I know not where that people arriving by bicycle would have 50 per cent knocked off their entrance fee. I thought we might qualify for a free ticket, or at least a cup of tea, having travelled hundreds of miles by horse to get there. What more ecologically friendly mode of transport could there be?

We followed the CAT signs and came to the bottom of the vernacular railway, via which people reached the centre. Two large car parks were almost full, so clearly plenty of people are ready to consider new ways of living for the next millennium. There was a decorative, babbling brook, which the horses dragged us towards, but sharp, if pretty, stones had been laid along its banks, making it impossible to get the horses anywhere near it. Disappointingly, there were no hitching posts and nothing else we could tie the horses to. I held them and Nan went in search of a bucket. She returned moments later with a nasty-looking plastic affair that had been used for washing the floor. Despite her best attempts to remove the smell of bleach, neither Sooty nor Holly would drink from it, however thirsty they were. We left the CAT feeling rather let down. Horses obviously aren't part of their plan for the future. There may be information on horsepower inside the centre, but as we couldn't tie the horses up anywhere and needed to get them to water, we weren't able to go in and find out.

The last few miles of a hard day always seem longer than the first. It took an age for us to reach the hamlet of Corris and turn right towards our destination of Foel Friog. This was slate country and everything seemed to be made of the stuff. Not only the roofs, but the walls of the houses too. Even the fences were constructed from heavy slate slivers. It is a stone which looks permanently wet to me, and a little gloomy.

We passed a field of shire horses – two mares, a foal and, I think, a stallion. They tore along the fence beside us, snorting like hippos. Holly was quite unnerved. The horses at Foel Friog were equally excited by our arrival, and executed some pretty impressive handstands. We were also greeted by five barking dogs of various breeds and flavours, all chained, straining against their ties, and making as much noise as possible. Jane came out of the farmhouse and spent so long talking to the dogs to shut them up we began to feel invisible.

She was a woman in her early twenties, shy and blonde. She looked at our horses. 'They're quite heavy, aren't they?' was her judgement.

'Well, they are cobs,' I said, rather surprised.

'Would you like to hose them off?' she asked.

We imagined how shocked they would be if we suddenly did such a thing to them. 'Oh no, thank you,' I said, 'they prefer to have a good roll.'

We put them in a flat paddock which had very little grass. Holly threw me a look as if to ask, 'Is this it, after twenty miles?' I promised her extra carrots in the morning.

Inside we glimpsed Jane's equally youthful husband. She was English, he Welsh, and they had recently bought the hundred-acre farm and three hundred sheep. I wondered how the locals had taken to these young interlopers.

We were given a large, pleasant room with a colour TV, and a window from which we could see the horses. We knew the nearest pub must be some distance away, and couldn't remember passing one since Machynlleth. Rather than have an evening meal, we asked Jane if it would be possible to have a sandwich. She said she would leave cold meat and bread out in the dining room and we could help ourselves, which sounded fine. She was a strange girl who tried to be helpful, but had an odd manner and a habit of coming into our room.

We checked the horses before going to bed. They had stood up to their hard day very well. Sooty's shoe looked good for a few more miles, and Holly's digestive system had calmed down a bit. Her rubs from the packs were getting larger and balder, but didn't seem to be sensitive. We realised how much we were going to miss our lovely mounts when we went home.

The dogs were mercifully quiet at night, and we fell asleep serenaded by a particularly tuneful owl.

Days Eighteen and Nineteen — Snowdonia!

I woke up screaming from a nightmare at half past five the following morning. Maybe it was the imminence of having to return to our real lives that caused it. It left me feeling unsettled and confused. My shrieks left Nan feeling like a nervous wreck. We were both wide-awake. We opted for a cup of tea and yesterday's crossword puzzle to take my mind off my bad dream. At seven o'clock we were still battling with twenty-four across, sipping our third cup of tea, and I was enjoying a cigarette. There was a knock on the door and Jane came in. She looked at us both sitting in the same bed, said that smoking wasn't allowed then disappeared again. I'm sure she read all sorts of inaccurate things into our being in the same bed, but I was more fed up about having to put out a perfectly good cigarette.

In the dining room she told us her husband was vehemently anti-smoking. We had obviously upset him as in the next room rock music was being played at very high volume. We passed on the cooked breakfast, not wishing to sit through half an hour of the noise we were being subjected to. Jane stood in front of me, wordlessly holding a piece of paper and shuffling from foot to foot.

'Is that the bill?' I asked, in an attempt to get things moving. She nodded, handed it to me, and left the room. I had known the price for staying at Foel Friog before I booked, but I was still horrified to see that one night had cost us £65. We had been charged the full evening meal price for our d-i-y sandwich, which I felt was unfair. Five pounds each for the horses would have been more reasonable if there had been any grass in the field. Still, it was done now. We hastened to pack, anxious to leave. As we tacked up the horses the music continued, only louder, so Mr Jones could hear it above the racket of the pressure hose he was using to wash his cars a few yards from us. I'm sorry if my smoking in our room upset him, but he has a lot to learn about how to treat paying guests, and ripping them off financially will not win him any friends either.

Jane had been helpful regarding our route, however, showing us how we could take what is now a cycle route through the mountains.

We rode through the slate village of Aberllefeni, where children ran after us squealing and flapping carrier bags. The horses ignored them. There is still a working slate quarry in the village. Deep holes mark the mountainside, spewing landslides of sharp, shiny slate from the belly of the hills. The dark pine trees, narrow valley and deep, grey-black of the stones were oppressive. We trotted up the short distance of lane and were pleased to soon be opening a gate onto the mountain.

The path was very rocky, making the horses pick their way carefully. We climbed up several hundred feet in less than two miles. The sun was hot again and the horses blew and sweated heavily. We paused to let them catch their breath. We had left the dark valley far below us now. The grass either side of the track was sparse and wiry. The sheep were once again hardy Welsh, small, tough and easily frightened. Buzzards wheeled above.

A further mile's climb brought us through the pass and presented us with dramatically spectacular scenery. Snowdonia, as far as we could see. The mountains lay ahead, rugged, sharp-edged and wild, like the spines of a sleeping dinosaur. In the far distance we could make out the lofty outline of Snowdon itself. Even the horses were im-

Sooty and Nan in Snowdonia

pressed, raising their heads, ears forward, responding to the timelessness of the place. Their ancestors might have run wild up here, growing their coats thick and long against the harsh winters, drinking from the crystal mountain streams, grazing on the tough grass that forced its way up between rock, heather, gorse and whinberry. A scientist once told me that, measured in the time scale of the evolution of stars and planets, the mountains were galloping. Indeed, that is precisely how they appeared. They were not static lumps of rock and soil, but moving, breathing entities, surging upwards and rolling on toward the horizon. You could almost hear them roar.

We descended slowly; absorbing our environment, and letting it absorb us. We crossed the main Machynlleth to Dolgellau road and continued along the cycle route. These routes can be negotiated on horseback, but they are not designated bridle paths, so you could find yourself up against a stile or narrow footbridge. We wouldn't have risked it if we hadn't been assured that another rider had been able to get through the week before. We were back on enclosed farmland now, and the small paddocks meant gates! Lots and lots of gates. You have to accept them as a reasonable price to pay for crossing private land, but a dozen or so in a couple of miles becomes pretty wearing. Especially when most of them cannot be opened from the back of a horse.

Nan resorted to walking, until she was driven back on board by deep mud. At one gateway we had to turn into cowgirls to prevent a boisterous bunch of bullocks diving through and joining us for the rest of the day's ride. The gates had the effect of slowing our progress considerably. In fact, it took us longer to cover eight miles than it had done to travel twice that in other places.

We found the lane marked on our map and trotted the mile or so to the Cross Foxes Inn. The horses slept, tied to a paddock gate under a shady tree, while Nan and I tucked into sandwiches and chips. Our toast breakfast had not lasted us many miles.

We ate in silence, aware that we were nearing the end of our journey. If circumstances had allowed we would happily have gone on for at least two more weeks, and I'm sure the horses could have, too.

A couple of miles easy hacking brought us to Fronoleu Farm Hotel. We rode across the car park and found the proprietor. 'We're booked in for a couple of nights,' I explained, 'the four of us.'

He looked a little surprised. 'That'll be my wife,' he said with a sigh. He found a field easily enough, however. There was plenty of

Near Lake Vyrnwy

thick, close grass, a small stream, some leafy trees, pale grey stone walls and a view to keep the horses entertained.

The hotel had good facilities, friendly, helpful staff and comfortable rooms. We wallowed in deep baths before changing into our non-riding clothes. It was nice to feel clean and fresh and feminine again. We sat in the lounge bar where a harpist was playing. We sipped long drinks from tall glasses and relished the squashy armchairs. The rooms were full of tack, pictures and paintings of horses, particularly Shires. These had worked the farm before it became a hotel.

The dining room was pretty and interesting, with a further collection of farming artefacts and memorabilia. We enjoyed delicious steaks – something of a speciality of the house. The wine, puddings and service were all good and we spent a lovely evening relaxing, and eating far too much.

It was bliss to have a lie-in the next morning, not to have to leap up and struggle with heavy packs. We ate a leisurely breakfast and decided just to hack the horses a couple of miles to stop them stiffening up. We would be spending another night at Fronoleu Farm Hotel before heading for home.

The horses appreciated the absence of their heavy saddlebags and walked out happily with long, easy strides. We enjoyed the freedom from the flapping, rustling packs, too. It was lovely to bowl along without coat or map, letting the road take us wherever it would. Surprisingly, or not, it took us to a pub, where we paused for rest and light refreshment. We didn't stay long as we found ourselves too easily becoming melancholy - thinking this was the last day of our journey, the last pub stop, and so on. We trotted home briskly, sensing the horses' confusion at the shortness and circular nature of the day's work. When I turned Holly loose in the field she stood and looked at me instead of putting her head down to eat straight away. Her expression said, 'Well, is this right, or are you going to tack me up again in a minute?'

Nan and I took a more modern form of transport to visit nearby Lake Vyrnwy. This is the largest reservoir in Wales and supplies water to Liverpool. It was constructed, like many such artificial lakes, in the nineteenth century. Five miles long, it is an impressive sight and an awe-inspiring feat of engineering. Every effort was made to make the lake appear as natural as possible, though this did little to appease the Welsh, who resented the English benefiting from cheap water at the expense of their valleys. Now, with tourism fast becoming the biggest industry in Wales, its value as a place of recreational activities and an undeniable beauty spot are justly expounded.

We walked along the shores of the lake, the choppy water lapping in quick waves against our feet. Again I was reminded of R.S. Thomas's intense dislike of reservoirs, with their drowned secret villages. If you want to enjoy these places you have to take them at face value, and not dip beneath the surface. We took tea and cat's tongues at the Lake Vyrnwy Hotel, which was a splendid vantage point. It provided a sheltered corner of Victorian luxury from which to view the prettier aspects of the lake.

Later, after another lavish meal at Fronoleu Farm Hotel, we sat in the field with the horses, watching them graze. The twilight had deepened and several stars studded the sky. The distant hills were silhouettes. We let our minds travel back over our journey, and pondered the behaviour of the horses. They had been taken from their home of more than a decade, ridden into the unknown for three weeks by two strangers, sleeping in a different bed every night. Their diet had been varied and unpredictable, and each day had presented them with new challenges. They had progressed from tiredness to sleek, shiny fitness, and, I believe, had come to truly enjoy the travel, progression and freedom of the journey as much as we had. They had been stoic and reliable, and had never frightened us. They had put up with the attentions of yet more strange people, and an assortment of other animals. They had endured long, hard days, bad weather, hot weather and heavy traffic without complaint. They had put up with the moods and caprices of their riders. And, every day, they had come willingly up to us for more of the same. We owed them such a lot, for, in the end, it was they who had made the journey safe and enjoyable. We continued to sit and watch them until their warm, friendly shapes merged with the darkness and melted into the night.

Days Twenty and Twenty-One –
Heading home

We woke to a grey but dry day and automatically climbed into our riding clothes. It was only as Nan was putting her boots on that we realised the spurs were no longer necessary. We took ages eating breakfast and packing our bags, trying to kill time as we waited for the lorry to arrive. We were both more than a little nervous about transporting the horses. As far as we knew, Sooty may never have been boxed before, and it was certainly a few years since Holly had. We didn't have a protective travelling boot or bandage between us, and no haynets to keep them occupied during the journey. In my experience, loading horses is one of the more dangerous parts of dealing with them, far more so then hacking. Accidents can happen in an instant, and are usually of the squashing variety. Nan had had trouble loading her own horse in the past, and so was dreading the whole thing. She knew I'd had to transport horses about quite a lot some years ago, so she was relying on me to make sure everything went smoothly. I did my best not to show how apprehensive I was.

The lorry arrived on time, and the young driver was relaxed and helpful. The vehicle was a medium-sized cattle truck, not swanky, but strong, stable, and with plenty of space. I asked the driver if he often transported horses. He looked a little uncomfortable as he told me he'd only ever taken them to be slaughtered. I decided Nan and the horses didn't need to know this.

As we reversed the lorry into the field adjoining the one the horses were in, Holly stopped eating and stared. In her youth she had been to all sorts of competitions, so she knew what was going on. We put some clean shavings on the floor and took out all the partitions. I reckoned that being confined in a small space would not go down well with Sooty, and might, given his dislike of stables, make him panic. We caught the horses and led them towards the lorry.

'Just follow me,' I told Nan as I walked in front of Holly with a slack rope, chatting away and trying to act as matter-of-fact as possible. I hoped nobody would notice me holding my breath. Holly didn't let me down. She walked up the steep, clattery ramp behind me and stood still while I tied her to one of our much-travelled pieces of string.

Sooty hesitated outside. He lowered his head to sniff the unfamiliar surface he was being asked to tread on, then walked quickly in after Holly.

'Good boy! Just tie him to the string, quick as you can,' I said to Nan, 'then nip out, but don't get directly behind him as you go.'

Seconds later we were outside with the ramp up and securely fastened. I breathed again. First phase over. We peered in through the air vents. Holly had already arranged herself sideways across the available space. Sooty looked puzzled. 'Right,' I said, 'let's get moving.'

Paul was a competent and careful driver, but we had some particularly bendy, mountainous roads to cover. I found myself frantically stamping my right foot on a non-existent break as we hurtled down hills into sharp bends. Every time we rounded a corner Nan and I exchanged worried glances. I knew exactly what was going through her mind. What would we find when we next lowered the ramp? I had visions of horses falling over, or at the very least treading on each other and themselves with their ironclad hooves.

The sweaty-palmed, noisy, stress-filled journey seemed interminable, but did, in fact, last two and a half hours. By the time we crept along the rough track to Nan's farmhouse I was exhausted from trying to appear calm and unperturbed. Glancing inside before letting them out we could see that Holly was still wedged across the width of the lorry, whilst Sooty was loose and roaming about. I had worked on the idea that he might feel less panicky if he wasn't restricted at all, and I had known he could easily break the string if he felt like it. Clearly, he had.

We lowered the ramp and peered in, hardly daring to look. Paul, happily unaware of our fears, marched in and led the horses out. They were completely unscathed. Not a mark or a bump or a scratch. Nan smiled for the first time in three hours. We turned the horses out in the grassy yard next to the house. True to form, they tucked in to the food on offer. We waved Paul goodbye, hauled our tack and bags inside, and poured ourselves a much-needed glass of wine.

Fearing the journey might have distressed the horses, we had arranged not to hack them back to their home until the following day. In fact, they didn't turn a hair, but Nan and I were glad of the rest. And the chance to clean our tack and find some fresh clothes. The next morning I sat at my bedroom window for a few moments watching the horses. This was to be the last day that I would wake up to see them waiting for me. The last day we would travel together. It was time to take them home.

We set off for the four-mile ride pack free, so lightly loaded but with heavy hearts. Saying goodbye to the horses was something we had tried not to think about, but now it had to be faced.

Whether or not the horses recognised their surroundings, I can't be sure, but they certainly knew they were going home. Sooty pulled hard, wanting to trot all the time. Holly threw her head about and shied at invisible demons. We trotted most of the road to Crickhowell to try and settle them, but it didn't make much difference. They were far too fit to be tired by a couple of miles trotting. We rattled through the small town in a rather rushed and undignified manner. The narrow road that led from Crickhowell to the stables covered a steep two miles, but the horses weren't going to be slowed down by anything now. We let them trot up most of it, then persuaded them to steady to a more sensible walk. The sun had come out and Nan and I quickly pulled off our coats, but the horses had barely broken a sweat and weren't blowing at all.

Moments later we crested a small hill, wiggled round a sharp left hand bend, and there were their stables. My mother and my niece, Amy, were waiting to welcome us home, as were Angela and one or two teenage helpers. Sooty and Holly had been much missed. After untacking them we lingered awkwardly, not wanting to leave, putting off the final moment. The horses stood together in the yard, happy and relaxed, for all the world as if they had just come back from a short hack. We gave them a parting carrot, promised to come back and visit them soon, and finally dragged ourselves away.

Postscript

It was very hard to settle back into anything like normal life after our return. It surprised me how, in just a few short weeks, riding, travelling, exploring, moving on every day had become the norm. We now seemed unsuited to anything else. Nan and I missed the horses terribly, too. A strong bond grows between horse and rider, particularly when they are facing new challenges together. For days after the trek I felt restless and unsettled, and loathed returning to the chaos and noise of London.

We learned that the horses were changed by their experiences too. They are now, understandably, inseparable, and will probably remain so forever. Sooty, once a bit of a baby, has now become a perfect lead horse, who simply loves being in front and setting the pace. He won't suffer fools now, though, and has been known to charge off with novices. Instead of plodding around with inexperienced people thumping his ribs or pulling at his mouth, he now enjoys lively outings with more ambitious riders. He also, I am told, has a tendency to turn into any pub car park he finds.

Holly has mellowed considerably. Her sweetened disposition and good manners make her such a pleasant mount that Angela herself now often chooses to ride her. Angela also said she had never seen the horses looking so sleek, fit and happy. It's wonderful to think they benefited from the trip in some way.

To anyone considering doing a ride such as ours I would say, don't hesitate, don't put it off or find obstacles or excuses – just do it! Naturally a certain amount of planning is important, and I hope that you will have gleaned some useful tips from our experiences.

Of course, there are some things I might do differently were I to plan another trek. A more comfortable saddle would be the first thing. Also, had time allowed, it would have been lovely to have organised a few local guides here and there to take us to places we didn't quite dare explore on our own. Those things aside, however, there's not much else I'd change. The mobile phone was useful, though it's a bad idea to rely on it. We were lucky enough not to have to use anything from our equine medical kit, but I wouldn't set out without one. Accurate map-reading is a skill that develops surprisingly quickly – getting lost or seriously miscalculating a ride distance steepens one's learning curve considerably.

I can't stress enough the importance of a suitable horse. Those lucky enough to own such beasts will be well aware of your own good fortune. Anyone tempted to take their much loved, beautiful, but traffic-shy, nervous or otherwise unreliable animal, should think again. Nan has her own adored horse, but wisely left him at home.

For me the trek was a tremendous experience. I was frequently touched by the kindness and friendliness of the people we met. I was impressed by, and grateful for, the behaviour of the horses. I was thrilled and moved by the glorious landscape of the country through which we travelled, and learned so much about its heart and its history. I sincerely hope that the future for this semi-wilderness is not as bleak as is being forecast at the time of writing. Nan and I agree that we also learned something about ourselves, and gained confidence from being self-sufficient and achieving our goal. When I started to plan the trek I had no horse, no money and eight weeks to organise everything in. It goes to show what you can do if you really want to. So go on, get the maps out and turn that dream into a reality. Good luck!

Useful Contacts

Angela Ralph, Llangenny Riding Centre, Llangenny, Crickhowell, Powys. Tel: 01873 810329

The White Hart, Talybont, Brecon, Powys. Tel: 01874 676227

Cantref Riding Centre, Brecon, Powys. Tel: 01874 665223

Megan Oswald, The Cwmysg Country House, Sennybridge, Powys. Tel: 01874 636396

The Lluest Trust, Beili Bedw, Llanddeusant, Llangadog, Carmarthenshire. Tel: 01550 740661

Plas Taliaris, Llandeilo, Carmarthenshire. Tel: 01558 823590

Anne Ryder-Owen, Fferm-y-Felin, Llanpumsaint, Carmarthenshire. Tel: 01267 253498

Carolyn Morgan, Crosswell Horse Agency, Iet Wen, Velindre, Crymych, Pembrokeshire. Tel: 01239 891262

The Golden Lion Inn, East Street, Newport, Pembrokeshire. Tel: 01239 820321

Shirley Muntz, Pontcarreg, Nevern, Pembrokeshire. Tel: 01239 820059

Evans Brothers Auctioneers, Llanybydder, Dyfed. Tel: 01570 480444

The Black Lion, Llanybydder, Dyfed. Tel: 01570 493208

Elinor Evans, Nantymedd Farm, Llanfair Road, Llanfair, Clydogau, Lampeter. Tel: 01570 493208

The Talbot Hotel, Tregaron. Tel: 01974 298208

The Black Lion Hotel, Talybont, Aberystwyth, Dyfed. Tel: 01970 832335

Fronoleu Farm Hotel, Tabor, Dolgellau, Gwynedd. Tel: 01341 422361

The British Horse Society, Stoneleigh Deer Park, Kenilworth, Warwickshire. Tel: 01203 690 676 (B&B for horses)

Trek King, 847 Fulham Road, London W9. Tel: 0171 736 5982

John Pritchard Transport. Tel: 01873 856338

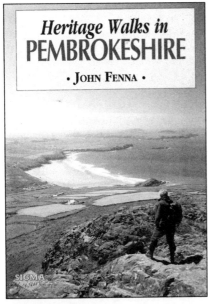

Also about Wales:

BEST TEA SHOP WALKS IN SNOWDONIA

Enjoy a leisurely ramble in Snowdonia and complete the experience with a scrumptious afternoon tea! 27 superb, circular walks from 3½ to 8 miles suitable for all ages and experience. Dorothy Hamilton's directions are accompanied by sketch maps, photographs and notes on local history and wildlife. £6.95

SNOWDONIA WALKS WITH CHILDREN

Nick Lambert has designed these 20, circular walks around flat valleys and gentle slopes. A special feature of this series is the narrative written 'just for the kids' which highlights sights, wildlife and history. £6.95

DISCOVERY WALKS IN CARMARTHENSHIRE

John Fenna shows that Carmarthenshire has a great variety of walking terrain - cliffs, high moorland, craggy hillsides and quiet farmland. Routes are clearly delineated, will suit all ages and experience, and include parking and refreshment listings. £6.95

HERITAGE WALKS IN PEMBROKESHIRE

Discover the pleasures of Pembrokeshire away from tourist honeypots "an ideal introduction to the rich natural, historic, industrial and legendary heritage of this land of contrasts." W.T.B. TRAVEL NEWS. £6.95

WALKS IN MYSTERIOUS WALES

Ley hunter and researcher Laurence Main has compiled a vast collection of folklore and walks for his readers. "An excellent book" GLAMORGAN GAZETTE. "Most informative" CAMBRIAN NEWS.£6.95

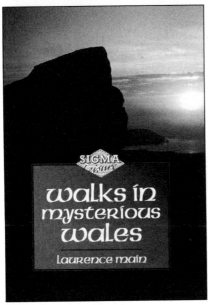